DISABUSING SEXUALITY

Canon Nathan Karema

authorHOUSE®

AuthorHouse™
1663 Liberty Drive
Bloomington, IN 47403
www.authorhouse.com
Phone: 1-800-839-8640

First published by AuthorHouse 07/15/2011

ISBN: 978-1-4567-7891-0 (sc)
ISBN: 978-1-4567-7892-7 (e)

Printed in the United States of America

DEDICATION

I dedicate this book to my son
Nathan Ndyamuhaki Karema (RIP)
for the care and love he had for the underprivileged.

ACKNOWLEGMENTS

I am grateful to all the people who have shared their time and knowledge with me and offered much needed support. Special appreciation is extended to Odira Karema, Modern Karema and Chris Karema for their invaluable contribution and support to the process and development of this book.

William Ahimbisibwes' contribution for the material in Chapter One, *Homosexuality,* is highly appreciated.

I very much appreciate Professor Laban Erapu's encouragement, his useful advice and his assistance on editing the final draft of the book.

Finally, I thank my Secretary, Irene Ninsiima, for the valuable time she devoted to typing and word-processing the drafts of this book.
Thank you all!

DISABUSING SEXUALITY
BY NATHAN KAREMA

DISABUSING SEXUALITY is an engaging exploration of all the various forms of sexual abuse that communities all over the world have to contend with. These range from the controversial and little talked about behavioural deviations like homosexuality to the more commonplace social tribulations like domestic violence, divorce, child abuse, rape, prostitution, substance abuse and the HIV/Aids pandemic, which considerably widens the reader's awareness of what amounts to sexual abuse.

Nathan Karema's book is not a scientific analysis even though it is medically well informed. It is not a moralistic invective although the author takes a bold stand on issues of sexual abuse. Its scope is extensive and its approach is informative. This book is for the layman and it appeals to the general reader who shares the author's concerns over the misconceptions that many people harbour about the various forms of sexual relationship. The tone of the book is critical but not judgmental. It seeks to explain what constitutes sexual abuse and goes on to recommend what needs to be done to correct these social anomalies.

One of the most outstanding features of the book is how

it endeavours to strip certain taboos off the subject of sexual abuse in order to bring these issues into the public domain for debate and discussion. The author asserts that it is through such open discourse that negative and harmful prejudices that abound regarding sexuality can be corrected. Knowledge then becomes a powerful weapon that can lead to the healing of the corrosive causes and damaging effects of sexual abuse.

Rape is one of the most prevalent forms of sexual abuse that the author convincingly argues is most poorly handled by the law enforcement agencies and the judiciary. He states that rape victims never receive justice because of the appalling attitudes of the police and the courts that treat victims like offenders who are harassed into proving the "alleged" crime beyond reasonable doubt. The complainants are scorned and treated with scepticism while the real wrongdoers are rarely convicted or at the most get away with the lightest of sentences. This results in rape victims choosing not to report to the police and that in turn results in the perpetrators becoming serial rapists who often commit the same crime with impunity because they know that they can lightly get away with it.

The position of women in society is of great concern to the author who devotes much of the book to demonstrating just how often women are the victims of all kinds of sexual abuse. He argues that in cases of domestic violence, whether it ends in divorce or not, it is more often the woman rather than the man who finds it harder to pick up the pieces and start anew. She has more to lose socially and economically in a male-dominated society in which she has to bear an unfair share of blame for the failure of the relationship. In general the woman is the weaker partner when it comes to negotiating sexual engagement. Women sometimes have no choice at all in the matter and that is why they are often forced into acts that they either resent or would not have accepted had their rights been considered on equal terms by the other party.

Nathan Karema's book succeeds in highlighting the fact that the right to amicable sexual relations is a prerequisite to creating a fair, just and healthy environment in which sexual abuse would not necessarily be eradicated but could be substantially reduced both in gravity and occurrence. His broad parameters for what constitutes sexual relations to be "disabused" may appear contentious to some readers because of their own sexual orientation or past experience, but that is precisely the concern the author is saying we should not sweep under the carpet but open up for debate.

Professor Laban Erapu
Bishop Stuart University
Mbarara—UGANDA

CONTENTS

FOREWORD

This book is about the many sexual abuses that society is plagued with all over the world with a special emphasis on Uganda, the author's home country. Written in a language that a layman can follow, the book is an informative discourse rather than a moralistic or judgmental denunciation. It is a courageous effort on a subject that many would consider taboo and tend to sweep under the carpet. Here it is all exposed and we the readers are made to have to deal with it in all its rawness. For people who have suffered sexual abuse, the succour here is the knowledge that they are not alone and they are not beyond help.

Overall the author's primary concern is for women and children whose comparative physical weakness in relation to men makes them susceptible to sexual harassment and other forms of abuse. Whether in marriage or in society at large, women are generally in a less advantageous position to insist on their rights or negotiate a fair deal that prevents them from being exploited by men.

The book covers most situations in which sexual abuse tends to happen, extending from homosexual relationships through divorce and rape to domestic violence. Virtually no area is untouched and the clear message that emerges is that sexuality is a dominant feature of man's life and its deviations have to be addressed as a matter of course.

The author identifies the problems and discusses

them in detail, enumerating cause and effect correlation, before offering solutions and remedies. The latter are put forward as suggestions that government and the various organisations that deal with victims of sexual abuse need to take heed of and make an effort to implement in order to eradicate the problem or reduce its abrasive repercussions on society.

Any kind of abuse needs to be negated or "disabused" as this book suggests. This is not the responsibility of any one individual or one group organisation alone: it is the problem of society as a whole. In the case of sexual abuse, there is a need for a change of attitude towards sex in society at large. For government and organisations that handle sexual abuse – particularly the police and the law courts – there is an urgent need to treat the victims of sexual abuse as humanely as possible and not with scepticism, disbelief and dismissive contempt. That is why rapists, for example, rarely get convicted while rape victims have to bury their shame and pain rather than report to authorities that will throw the burden of proof back at them. This only adds insult to injury and justice is denied to those who need it most while the perpetrators walk away to commit the same heinous crimes with impunity, knowing the law can never catch up with them.

This book calls to be read by anyone who has ever felt concerned about the laxity with which sexuality is treated in the so-called liberal society in which the rights of women and children in particular tend to be ignored or underrated when the rights of the individual in general are lauded. The author takes us from the public and societal domain, where these issues are often debated and theorised, to the real world where the practical solutions to the many problems raised by issues of sexual abuse usually lack force and sometimes favour men when they are the perpetrators.

Professor Laban O Erapu
Bishop Stuart University
Mbarara-Uganda

PREFACE

In this book, Mr. Karema has presented us with a sociological typology or inventory of current and un doubtable intractable social problems which if not addresses with determination and commitment may lead to social, economic and political stagnation, if not to anomie and social disorganisation.

The rate of social change that has been taking place in post colonial Africa has been so rapid that the majority of the new leaders were quite unable to know what to do. This inability to adequately address pressing social, economic and political problems explains the common hostility political leaders of opposition parties but also any one who herb ours anti- establishment views.

Some of the topics Mr. Karema has addressed are what sociologists refer to as social problems. An issue, such as drunkenness, corruption or rape is considered a social problem if and when it goes beyond the normal tolerance range, and the public begins to call for immediate official intervention.

Some of these problems are also not only deviant behaviour, but also criminal. For example, homosexuality, in some countries, is not a deviant behaviour but also a crime, and in some countries, it is regarded as a crime without victims. In some jurisdictions, prostitution is not a crime but a social service which simply requires state supervision and consequently, prostitutes are given acceptable titles such as sex workers and are required by law to have a license just like any traders in the market.

Social change if unguided or misguided may cripple the entire society. Poverty, one of the major characteristics of abrupt social change in third world countries should constitute a priority concern for the majority of African leaders.

Mr. Karema deserves our appreciation for the courage he exhibited in writing this book; for writing books has eluded many African leaders including intellectual elites. The art and interest in writing and reading books is not yet part of the African culture. It must be considered unfortunate to note that for a population of Ankole and Kigezi which is about five million not a single book is written either in Runyankole or English in a year. Political leaders should encourage people to write books, if social economic and political progress is to be achieved.

Prof. Mwene Mushanga, PhD

Chapter One

HOMOSEXUALITY:

Unmasking the Pleasures of Sin

Preamble

It is a Tuesday evening and I have just returned home after a hard day's work. I realize that I am in time for the nine o'clock news and I immediately tune in to my favourite broadcast: NTV Tonight.

The topical issue is Homosexuality. The gays have just won a case of human rights abuse against the Government for being assaulted by policemen who found them cuddling in public and decided to apprehend them.

The Minister of State for Ethics and Integrity is whimpering and ranting at the state of affairs in our dear motherland. What actually catches much of my attention is what one of the societal opinion leaders says.

Asked for a comment about the state of affairs, Rev Dr John Senyonyi, a renowned theologian from the Uganda Christian University, Mukono, proclaims: "this is a sin of our times, our ancestors had their own!"

That sent me racking my brain to discover what homosexuality really is, what causes it, how long it has existed, whether it is a choice and a number of other questions as shall be seen below.

What is Homosexuality?

I cannot go on without trying to find a universally acceptable meaning of homosexuality. Even before you jump to your favourite dictionary to try and get the definition, something is crystal clear. This word originates from a combination of two words, i.e. Homo and Sex.

At this stage I must be bringing to mind what your Biology teacher taught you about classification of mammals with man being referred to by the Latin word "Homo".

All this may be right. However, there is something else that we need to get more clearly: the word homosexuality stems from the Greek word "homos" which means "same". To put it crudely, homos-sex therefore means sex between people of the same gender. Indeed the e-based free encyclopaedia – Wikipedia refers to homosexuality as "*an enduring pattern of or disposition to experience sexual affection, or romantic attraction primarily to people of the same sex.*"

Therefore, a female who is attracted to a fellow female or a male who is attracted to a fellow male can both be said to have homosexual feelings.

In the modern era, however, to make homosexuality more acceptable, those who advocate for the rights of the homosexuals coined new nouns for each sex, i.e. Gay for males and Lesbian for females, arguing that the word "homosexual" as a noun is derogatory and does not carry the romantic connotations claimed by people of the same sex who have an immense desire for each other.

Man as a Sexual Being

Some scholars and activists for such people advocate that homosexuals should not be thought of in sexual terms. Hence, to focus my definition on sexual activity is not to think of homosexuals thus, but even if it were so, we all agree that where an emotive relationship is involved, there is a very strong likelihood of sexual activity. Therefore, for any one to try to divorce the two is to try to deny the reality of life.

To be more precise, to view homosexuality through the mirror of their sexual activity does not mean to merely caricature them in terms of their sexual activities. I generally agree that they do have life beyond "sex" but it is also paramount to understand that it may be very difficult to talk about humanity as a whole without referring to "sex". The reason is simple: Man is created as a sexual being to the extent that "Sex" is the only acceptable norm through which procreation is realised.

I have heard some homosexuals say that, whatever importance sex has for the heterosexual, it has the same importance for the homosexual. However, I would like to categorically reject such reasoning. To say that a homosexual has all the interests (even in sex) as a heterosexual has is to go overboard. If it were so, then I have to worry for future generations and especially with regard to continued existence of family.

This leads me to explain what God's purpose for sex is even though my topic is Homosexuality. When God created Adam and Eve, he was very clear in His instruction: "go ye multiply and fill the earth…" (Genesis 1:28). He knew that Adam and Eve would be able to multiply and equipped them not only with the necessarily body reactions like emotions, but in His wisdom He gave each of them the necessary part on their body that would compliment a part of the other so that they would be in position to bring forth other human beings.

Indeed humans have obeyed God's command that any right thinking individual who gets married at one time or another wants a child of their own. In some cultures, especially in Africa, bringing forth children is the main motivation for marriage.

Are homosexuals able to obey this command of God? Can two homosexuals bring forth a child? Your answer should be as good as mine.

How then can one say that the interests of heterosexuals and homosexuals are the same? How can homosexuals love in the divine image? To carry out Artificial Insemination in order for one to have a child is to simply tell God that

He is no longer necessary in the completion of the cycle to bring forth life. That would negate the need for God and the family.

I now rest this argument so as to move forward, for it would require a whole chapter just to elaborate on God's purpose for sex.

The Monkey Mind and the Pleasure Syndrome

Having desecrated the meaning of sex beyond recall, many homosexuals and their activists argue that the only means through which they can get maximum pleasure is through homosexual relationships. Indeed an article ran by *Red Pepper*, suggested that the reason why many women are turning to Lesbianism is because they no longer get enough sexual satisfaction from their male counter parts. I want to equate such reasoning to that of a monkey.

When you have a monkey and you throw it up a mango tree, chances are that in a few minutes you will have over fifty barely tasted but not eaten mangoes on the ground. That is not because the monkey finds one mango less sweet than another but out of sheer curiosity. The monkey will want to extract pleasure from every mango within its reach, discarding it as soon as it reaches out for the next.

I believe homosexuals who raise the pleasure argument are like that. When God created human beings, He did it so that men and women's physical natures could compliment each other's. That is to say, male and female to gain as much pleasure as they could with each other. This can be explained by the body language of two individuals (male and female) who have "turned on" each other. The man is supposed to have some of his body part(s) erect while on the contrary the woman is supposed to be more receptive by having some part of her body that is ready to be pleasurably penetrated.

In the case of homosexual intercourse, one hears that the other is left whimpering like a wounded dog after the act. Is this what is called pleasure? Even though my knowledge of biology may be limited, I have heard it said that the rectum should not be tampered with or else the affected person may face the bitter consequences. In the event that one's rectum being invaded regularly, on top of the several chemical lubricants that have to be forcefully pushed onto it, what will happen? I bet manufacturers of pampers are being pressured to turn to making adult pampers to cater for victims of homosexual intercourse.

If it were not for the monkey mentality, how would one opt to leave pleasure that produces positive results – procreation – and go for the pleasure that leaves one in pain, sorrow and disillusionment? To endure such pain is not love but sacrifice for the sexual gratification of the partner. When the name of the game is self-gratification, any outlet will do. I call this lust. It is only lust that seeks release in whatever outlet presents itself.

Why is this so? The opposite of love is not hatred; it is exploitation since it implies using someone merely as a means to an end. This is what lust leads homosexuals into doing.

Is Homosexuality the Sin of our Time?

As earlier quoted, the Rev Dr Senyonyi noted that this is one of the evils of our time. I however harbour a different view altogether. While this evil practice may have come out clearly in this century, it does not necessarily portray a sign of the end of time as many preachers seem to suggest. This Evil has existed for long through generation to generation in fact in my view it can be traced as far back as the time when Man sinned and tried to hide his nakedness from God in the Garden of Eden. I will explain what I mean by this. Assuming that you all know the myth of creation and the fall of man (Genesis 1 and 2), you will remember that the sinning of man marked the path of sin into the world. It is at that moment that sin becomes something that man was to struggle with until death. If you look at homosexuality as a sin, then you ought to realize that this evil too has co-existed with man from the time of our first ancestors, Adam and Eve. You may also want to remind yourself that as soon as Eve ate the fruit and gave to it to Adam who did the same, they were quick to realize that they were naked and they wrapped themselves with leaves around the loins; (Genesis 3:6-7) This shows us clearly that even before they could think of their disobedience to God, they had already been filled by lust and could not bear the sight of each other's nakedness, a thing they had never minded before sinning. Where did the shame come from? If you are Ugandan like me, you must have seen several Video clips of homosexuals at a Conference in the city with their faces masked and covered up with all sorts of materials to prevent the viewers from identifying them. Unlike Adam and Eve, these Ugandan Homosexuals are fully clothed but filled with shame. Hence, if you will agree with me that homosexuality is sin, then you should also agree that it is not a twenty-first century invention but has co-existed with mankind since creation.

To add to the above, the Bible shocks us with a clear view of Homosexuality. In the Old Testament, I came across a verse that explains this clearly:

"If a man lies with a man as one lies with a woman, both of them have done what is detestable. They must be put to death; their blood will be on their own heads." (Leviticus 20:13).

This does not need any explanation. The writer of Leviticus shows us that there the evil of Homosexuality existed in his time or else he would never have bothered to write anything about it. In the New Testament, I was shocked to read how the Corinthians engaged in homosexuality. In his first letter to these people St. Paul implores thus:

"Do you not know that the wicked will not inherit the kingdom of God? Do not be deceived: Neither the sexually immoral nor idolaters nor adulterers nor male prostitutes nor homosexual offenders nor thieves nor the greedy nor drunkards nor slanderers nor swindlers will inherit the kingdom of God." (1 Corinthians 6:9-10).

When we look at St. Paul and his writings, we are looking at more than 2000 years back. Therefore, the evil of homosexuality is not one that has just cropped up in the last century.

Looking at our own societies, I was shocked to learn of the bitter realities when I mounted a search for information about this evil in the African societies. Before I go to several societies in which homosexuality was traced, let's look at our own society in Uganda. One Sunday afternoon while watching a talk show hosted by Mr. Gawaya Tegule on NTV, a Lesbian and homosexual rights activist – Jeninah Namukasa (not real name) – asked a question which to me made sense even when I do not have room for homosexuality. She queried the pastor with whom she was hosted where *okusiyaga,* the Luganda word for homosexual had come from if the practice was alien. I thought her question was not given due justice. It left me perplexed, could the allegations that Kabaka Mwanga wanted to "homosex" the palace pages that were later burnt to death and are now The Uganda Martyrs be true? If it is true, is it the Kabaka alone that had such disordered desires or could the practice have been existent in the society at the time?

Leaving Uganda at that, revelations of homosexuality in the ancient and middle age period are shocking. The first homosexual couple to be sighted on African soil is said to have been seen around 2400 BC. This Egyptian couple is commonly regarded as Khnumhotep and Niankhkhnum. The pair is portrayed in a nose-kissing position, the most intimate pose in Egyptian art. This practice was widespread from continent to continent and from generation to the next till the present day. Hence, the evil of homosexuality is not merely a sin of our time, but our era has given it newness. We are living in sophisticated days, our technological advances are unbelievable and it is such scientific discoveries that have made this evil much more popular than ever before. Take for example the internet; we are able to find out anything with the click of a mouse. It is not uncommon for thousands of youth as well as adults to surf pornographic literature. As if that was not bad enough, they go further to specifically surf homosexual pornography. This is what creates a difference between homosexuality in the 15th century and today.

Is Homosexuality a Human Right?

This is a very noble question that sparks debate wherever it is raised. In Uganda, most if not all the people who advocate for the legalization of Homosexuality hinge their arguments on this pillar. Even in countries beyond our borders the human rights talk is the only channel through which homosexuals and their advocates can place their needs to legislative bodies. For instance, the Malawi Human Rights Resources Centre in its November 2005 proposal stated thus:

"This is a recognised international human rights standard. Discrimination of persons in many forms is prohibited and all persons are, under any law; guaranteed equal and effective protection against discrimination on grounds of race, colour, sex, including sexual orientation."

This seems to suggest that the heterosexual people are abusing the right of the homosexual to determine their own sexual orientation. But my question is: what is a human right? In a layman's language, a human right is a fight against evil. As the above quotation suggests, our fathers who fought hard for the promulgation of human rights must have intended to safeguard freedom and respect for all individuals on the globe, no matter what. However, I have a question to put forward: is homosexuality a human right?

Let us consider this analogy, if I have an enemy who has tortured me so much and I have the opportunity to retaliate, should I kill this person? If I did, I would be setting myself free from the torture inflicted on me by this enemy. But is it right? If this doesn't make sense, allow me to use another scenario. We all have a right to shelter, but do we go sleeping anywhere we find? Why are there offences like trespass? You have a biological right to pass out excreted food from your body at any time, but can you allow yourself to be seen defecating in the middle of a street or in the middle of your sitting room simply because it is your right?

What I am labouring to explain here is that I think while one has rights to do as they please, these rights should not extend to the absurdities. In my understanding, an anus was created to pass out waste and never for the pleasurable experience of intercourse as the Gays seem to find it. To do so is to change the world order which in itself is tantamount to trespassing on other people's rights. That someone has a right to do as they please does not mean they should kill, trespass, commit adultery, "homosex" or sleep with a dog just because they find pleasure in that.

The talk about homosexuality for whatever reason deserves no room for discussion in view of human rights. To do so is to deny the original ideals of human right activists.

Speculations into Causes of Homosexuality

Trying to determine what really causes homosexuality can be the most challenging task. Many people simply do not know what causes homosexual inclinations. Many others believed the erroneous theory that homosexuality is solely biological while many others mistakenly believe it is a choice. Typically, the biological explanation is preferred by homosexuals as this explanation helps to generate greater tolerance and also helps to build their case for minority status. However, while looking at these causes, we ought to examine them very critically without necessarily being judgmental. The sole reason for trying to share this element of the causes is to assist us to understand the root of the evil so that those who are hooked into it will know the truth and the truth will set them free. For those who have the inclinations to the evil, they will find a solution. Those who are vehemently opposed to the evil like me, will learn to educate the rest of the population with no bias.

Today, society seems to believe in only two popular explanations: either people are born gay, or else it is a choice. Unfortunately, however, we ought to be aware that neither of the two widely held beliefs provides a comprehensive explanation for the origins and hence causes of homosexuality.

While homosexuality is not simply biologically based, neither are homosexual attractions a conscious choice. Attractions and desires are like feelings; they come from deep within us and are not a conscious choice. Nobody ever chooses to cry when they lose their loved ones, it just comes naturally and the feelings I am talking about are like that. Furthermore, the idea that same sex attractions are a choice is extremely offensive, inconsiderate and harmful to those who have these desires. Promoting the perspective that it is a choice will never solve the problem but will perpetuates the stigma and intolerant attitudes that exists towards homosexuals.

The Biological Argument

There are a number of possible explanations for the popularity of the biological argument, especially among the homosexuals themselves. Certainly, if there are only two options, that it is biological or that it is a choice, it is clear that the biological option would be the preferred option, especially in an era when anything that promotes greater tolerance is more widely accepted. The goal of the homosexual brethren in insisting that they posses a gene that influences them to become attracted to people of their sex is just that – the desire be socially accepted by the other members of society. The biological explanation is used to gain that acceptance. It is assumed that if homosexuality is strictly physiological, society will be more compassionate and tolerant towards homosexuals.

Most homosexuals will not entertain the idea that the practice is not biologically driven since any other explanation is often perceived as a threat to their cause. Therefore, whereas such a view may be effective in the promotion and widespread acceptance of such people, it is incomplete and misleading. As far as we are concerned, there is no scientific evidence that clearly states that there are men who have hormones that make them attracted to other men or women with hormones that make them attracted to other women. Hence, to base oneself on such a biased opinion held by those who benefit from it as a whole truth is tantamount to suicide.

Believing homosexuality is biologically based is actually quite limiting to homosexuals, and therefore has negative implications. For homosexuals who are not happy with the gay lifestyle, the biological explanation gives no hope for any other option. It suggests that since they were born homosexual, there is no possible means through which they can reform and develop normal heterosexual feelings and this is not true. There are many homosexuals who have reformed and returned to normal heterosexual life and there are thousands of others who are discontented with the practice and are looking for a way out.

The Argument on Choice

If you interact with homosexuals, chances are that they would not want to be associated with the theory that they chose to be gay or lesbian consciously. They are more comfortable with the escapist view that they were born just like that. They have always argued that no one would choose to be something that could cause them to be scorned by society, rejected by their families, and considered as hard core criminals in societies where being homosexual is totally unacceptable and could be punishable by life imprisonment just like in Uganda.

However, some homosexuals – especially those who were once married – do believe that it is by their conscious choice that they are homosexuals. A good example is the three time basket ball gold medallist at the Olympics, Sheryl Swoopes. In an exclusive Interview on Gay.com she comments very clearly that it is by choice that she got attracted to a fellow woman and decided to "come out" and proclaim it. However, as I shall discuss later, I do not look at it as a simple choice for a woman to become a lesbian. It is a displacement of ill feelings towards men by transferring affection to a fellow woman who may prove to be more receptive. Therefore, even those who seem to diverge from the main view of homosexuals – that it is a result of biological factors – seem to have plunged into the habit due to factors beyond a simple decision as they may assume. It is important at this time to delve deeper into what may be the real cause of Homosexuality.

The Argument on Environmental Factors

There has not been any conclusive scientific research into the real causes of homosexuality. Those that have attempted to define this all seem inconclusive, depending on who commissioned the study. However, some psychologists like Julie Harren have tried to study the behaviour of many homosexuals and came up with likely causes through their observations. Given a fair consideration, these psychological hypotheses may prove better speculative methods than the researches done. In the view of such psychologists, environmental factors can best explain the practice of same sex attractions.

The Parenting Factor

To begin with, Julie Harren explains the various developmental needs children have, especially the need for connection with the same-sex parent and same-sex peers. She explains that children are not simply born with a sense of their own gender but that their gender identity is formed through connections and interactions with others, primarily members of the same sex. She further holds that children look first to their same-sex parent and then to same-sex peers to form their own identity: to understand how they measure up, how they fit in, what value they have as boys or girls, what it means to be male or female, etc. When children do not form healthy same-sex bonds and their needs for same-sex connection go unmet, these needs do not go away; they simply intensify or take on another form. Typically, near puberty, these unmet needs take on a sexual form, the emotional needs become sexualized (Satinover, 1996). These developmental factors, combined with genetic temperament, which impacts perceptions, all go into the development of homosexuality.

In her submission, psychologist Julie Harren seems to agree with B.A. Robinson of the Ontario Consultants on religious tolerance that: "if the child is unable to form a loving relationship with the parent of the same gender, the child would take this incompleteness into adulthood, where he would continue to seek love from another adult of the same gender." This therefore suggests that children who are brought up by a single parent are very much likely to become homosexual compared to those who were brought up by both parents. While this is a contentious issue, you and I will agree that there is a marked difference between the behavior of children who were brought up by both parents and those that were brought up by single parents. It is common for boys who were taken care of by single mothers to have effeminate tendencies and for girls brought up by single fathers to be tomboys. However, this is not to suggest that such people are homosexual but to show the likely difference in their behavioral patterns which may stimulate such misplaced desires as same sex attractions.

Other Factors

Factors such as sexual abuse or traumatic experiences may also contribute to the formation of same-sex attractions. This is where the likes of Sheryl Swoopes lie. In her case, the trauma of divorce is the motivation behind her later sexual orientation. As the psychologists suggest, the way a human being is treated impacts much on their social behavior. In fact there is a popular saying that the outside of a person is a manifestation of his/her inner reality. In other words, if a person has a wounded mind and soul, they would rain down anguish, agony, distress and pain whenever they speak about what wounded them. Trauma like that of divorce can greatly impact on the life of its sufferer.

When I talk about sexual abuse I mean both self abuse like in masturbation and in external abuse like molestation and sodomy. To begin with, let me explain how external abuse leads to same sex inclinations. You may have heard rumours that there is homosexuality in schools. If you have not then I implore you to talk nicely to your child whether girl or boy and you will be shocked by the revelations, more so if your child is in a single sex school.

For example, I talked to Moses (not his real name) a former student of a school in Masaka which was plagued by homosexuality in the early 1990s. He told me that when he joined senior one together with tens of other children, none of them knew about the practice of *okwigula butu* (sodomy) as it was popularly known. Before long the senior students had identified those boys who by "luck" had been endowed with features like those of their sisters and they would force them into sodomy in dark corners.

What shocked me to the marrow was that before long, those who had been forced into sodomy grew to like it and they would eagerly look for their "partners" whenever they felt the desire for sex. I hope this is bamboozling but it would happen and the former culprits would take centre position to recruit new pupils when such pupils first reported in school and the cycle would continue. Moses told me of an event that the school was to be visited by a sister school, those who had identified themselves with sodomy would never surface as they regarded the visit as a competition. Before long, the practice spread like a bush fire until the media intervened. These boys would reach an extent of forgetting their identity and dressing like girls. The big possibility is that such people could have grown to live as homosexuals or they may have found an older person, "one like them", who talked them into getting out of it. For all intents and purposes I prefer the latter.

In addition to the above, Dr. Paul Cameron of Family Research Institute of Colorado Springs seems to agree with the view that, "touch the devil and you will never let go" in his article on what causes homosexual desire and can it be changed? He says one of the profound causes of such desires is "any homosexual experience in childhood, especially if it is a first sexual experience or with an adult". In an instance that such a child never finds one of its kind, he/she may live under the dilemma of a hen (homosexual) when he/she could fly and eat up hens (heterosexual).

Talking about self sexual abuse like masturbation, it too can be a serious motivation to disordered feelings and desires of a homosexual nature. How does that happen? This practice of masturbating is said to be one of the most addictive habits and once one starts they never stop until they do so by God's grace. It has also been discovered that this practice comes with several negative consequences including family break down just after one is married, selfishness, inferiority complex and more so towards the opposite sex and several others which I will extrapolate later when I talk about masturbation. Just in case a young person, male or female, is caught up in this habit, proper association and bonding with the rest of society becomes very difficult for them. In many instances such people only find it comfortable to associate with the people of their sex. Because they have a problem of bonding with the opposite sex, should a homosexual environment present itself, they will usually fall victim.

Seclusion of Same Sex People

While the dangers of secluding same sex people together for a long time may have been embedded in the above views, it is important to look at it independently. This is only to support the view that human beings can easily adapt to the environment in which they are placed. While seclusion appears a weak reason to rouse homosexual feelings, it has often done so due to the frustration that those placed in such secluded situations undergo. If you have been "behind bars" or talked to a person who has been there, they must have shared with you some of the nasty ordeals they underwent. Reports clearly indicate that homosexuality is practiced in places like prisons. This is not because the prisoners were homosexual before incarceration but it is simply due to the frustration of unfulfilled sexual desire that they don't expect to fulfill in the near future. Before long their lust erupts and anybody, whether man or woman, will want to have a moment of pleasure. This could also explain why children in single sex schools seem to be more susceptible to catch the "disease" than those in mixed schools where just being with children of the other sex appears to offer a sufficient measure of fulfillment.

In a society that highly esteems freedom of choice, we should concentrate on telling those who are already engaged in the habit the truth so that they can seek change if they so desire. The deeper understanding of homosexuality rather than mere criticism and attack of those who haven fallen victim to it will offer more options and increased hope both for the individuals concerned and their families as a whole.

Homosexuality and Health

If there is anything that has not been taken seriously, it is the health risk factors that come with homosexual practices. In one way or the other, this will have a great toll on the family if the debate to legalise homosexuality were to be globally successful.

HIV/Aids Risk

The cardinal truth is that the risk of disease incidence among homosexuals is so high that if a slightly larger proportion of the world's proportion caught up with the habit, there would be an urgent need for a new approach to disease control. That is because the level of promiscuity among homosexuals is unbelievably high, as evidenced by various publications.

In 2004, for example, the prominent medical website, WebMD, stated that men who have sex with both men and women are a "significant bridge for HIV to women" as established by the Centres for Disease Control. In 2003 alone, the Centres for Disease Control found that of newly diagnosed HIV infections in the United States, an estimated 63% were among men who were infected through sexual contact with other men. This in effect tells us that male homosexual acts such as anal sex account for a large proportion of HIV transmissions among the homosexuals around the globe. At this rate, where would we be heading to just in case we are to say yes to homosexuality? In Uganda too, even though there is lack of proper evidence, it is clear that the number of HIV/ Aids cases reportedly transmitted through homosexual acts is astronomical.

While the spread of HIV among homosexuals is on the increase, what puts the family at even a bigger risk is the life expectancy of homosexuals. Studies done by researchers at St. Paul's Hospital in Vancouver to assess how HIV infection and Aids is impacting the mortality rates for homosexual and bisexual men arrived at the alarming conclusion that life expectancy for gay and bisexual men of twenty is eight to twenty years less than the normal average for men. If the same pattern of mortality continues, it is estimated that nearly half of the gay and bisexual men currently aged 20 years will not reach their 65th birthday. Under the most liberal assumptions, gay and bisexual men in this urban centre are now experiencing a life expectancy similar to that experienced by all men in Canada in the year 1871. Unless one's heart is made of stone, this is a nasty finding.

Anybody with a clear mind doesn't want himself in such harm's way. With such percentages, there is a likelihood that in about one hundred years, we shall be having a much reduced number of young men able to foster Gods call – the call to multiply and fill the earth so that we can subdue it.

Other Maladies

Leaving the HIV threat aside, there are more maladies that have been closely associated with the homosexual practices. Of particular concern is anal cancer. According to Daling et.al the risk of anal cancer soars by 40 percent among those who engage in anal intercourse. I do hope that this is self-explanatory. Where is the future of the family with almost all homosexual men plagued by anal cancer?

The list of diseases resulting from such homosexual behaviour is almost endless. It has been learnt that more other infections such as these are associated with homosexuals: Chlamydia trachomatis, cryptosporidium, giardia lamblia, herpes simplex virus, human papilloma virus (HPV) or genital warts, isospora belli, microsporidia, gonorrhea, viral hepatitis types B & C, syphilis, etc.

Mental Health

Over the years in Kampala and in many other towns in Uganda, the number of insane people seems to be reaching significant heights. Psychiatrists attribute this to drug and substance abuse. But I am forced to add that this kind of substance abuse is engineered by practices like homosexuality. I do not intend to be vindictive but according to established knowledge, homosexuals have a substantially greater risk of suffering from psychiatric problems like suicide, depression, bulimia, antisocial personality disorder, and substance abuse. In a study published in a Journal of Consulting and Clinical Psychology, a national survey of female homosexuals found that 75 percent of the 2000 respondents had pursued some kind of psychological counselling and many of them had received treatment for long-term depression or sadness. While the female homosexuals seemed rather protected from diseases like anal cancer, the results of such a survey reveal that these lesbians are actually generally more ill than their male counterparts. Such an abnormality hitting directly at the would-be mothers of the nation leaves the future of our families and societies only in the hands of God.

Most homosexual rights activists attribute such psychiatric problems to the discrimination and intolerance the homosexuals receive from societies that are homophobic. On the contrary, however, a study done in Netherlands disapproves of such insinuations. Netherlands is one of the countries in the Western World in which homosexuals have free association to the extent that they can even legally marry.

Biblical View of Homosexuality

Several Biblical scholars have for long tried to justify the view that homosexuality is a sin and therefore disorderly and not acceptable in a society of believers. These scholars have faced stiff resistance by liberals and "free- minded" secularists. But even before I look at Biblical scenarios that clearly point to homosexuality as antisocial and hence sinful, I am struck by the immunological scientific point of view of Homosexuality. This scientific view clearly supports the Christian View that homosexual acts are intrinsically chaotic and hence contrary to the natural law. The body itself considers homosexual acts to be lawless. For instance, there are substances in seminal fluid called "immuno-regulatory macromolecules" that send out "signals" that are only understood by the female body, which will then permit the "two in one flesh" intimacy required for human reproduction. When deposited elsewhere, these signals are not only misunderstood, but cause sperm to fuse with whatever somatic body cell they encounter. This fusing is what often results in the development of cancerous malignancies. This illustrates how clearly the danger of muddled desire is not merely founded upon prejudice but rooted in science.

Looking at Biblical times, God clearly was enraged by homosexuality and pronounced punishment upon a people who were practicing such acts. In Genesis 19 we see God destroying Sodom and Gomorrah for wanting to have sex with the two male Angels that were being hosted by Lot. It is clearly written in chapter 19:5 "where are the men who came to stay with you tonight? Bring them out to us! The men of Sodom wanted to have sex with them". Despite Lot's offer of his two virgin daughters, the men of Sodom insisted that they wanted their fellow men. Consequently, the whole city was ablaze the next morning. This story is not to be used to threaten the people who are caught in the racket of homosexuality but should show the relevance of the Christian teaching against such a practice.

Leviticus seems to sum up the whole argument about homosexuality and Christianity. In 18:22 it says "No man is to have sexual relations with another man, God hates that." This is self-explanatory. To do the opposite is to openly say you detest God. For a section of the church to say they are homosexual and servants of God, is to consider God a double dealer, something that he will never be. He is not man that he should lie. He hates the practice. It should remain very clear that God does not say he hates the homosexual, he simply hates Homosexuality.

In Leviticus 20:13, God further warns his people on homosexuality. He says "if a man has sexual relations with another man, they have done a disgusting thing, and both shall be put to death. They are responsible for their own death." To put these men to death is to show the rest of the community that the practice of homosexuality is prohibited and hence they should try hard to avoid it. When God says that such people shall be responsible for their own death, it can be interpreted that God has given us (human beings) the power to know what is good and bad but that we own the responsibility to always strive for what is right. This can be linked to the New Testament teaching on homosexuality. St. Paul in his first letter to the Corinthians 6:9-10 says; "surely you know that the wicked will not possess God's kingdom. Do not fool yourselves; people who are adulterers or homosexual perverts or who steal or greedy or drunkards or who slander others or are thieves – none of these will possess God's Kingdom." You will agree with me that not to possess the Kingdom of God is to die. This is what leaves room for those who are already engaged in the practice of homosexuality. There is hope that if such people repent, they can still avoid death and gain possession of God's Kingdom which each believer is looking up to.

Other Religious Beliefs

One also needs to understand whether Christianity alone has no room for homosexuality. The fact is that there is no religious sect that seems to agree with homosexuality unless homosexuals have their own religious sect. Islam, for example, comes out very clearly to condemn the practice. The Koran speaks of homosexuals thus: "We also sent Lût; he said to his people: 'Do you commit adultery as no people in creation (ever) committed before you? For you practice your lusts on men in preference to women: you are indeed a people transgressing beyond limit".

In this example, the prophet Lût is reprimanding the people who are involved in homosexual acts. This solidifies the view that Islam considers homosexuality a great sin and an evil punishable under the Islamic law.

There is therefore no refuge for homosexuals in any religion except in the many human movements that propagate such ideals as secularism, humanism, the scientific method and the general view of atheism.

Conclusion

Like its sister – prostitution – homosexuality existed, exists and will continue to exist in future as long as uncontrolled desires exist. The two survive in this way. Homosexuals should recognize and admit that their advocators who promise an erotically charged transcendence through same-sex relationships have rightly discerned that human beings are desiring creatures. They have figured out the way to their hearts because they 'get it': they rightly understand that, at root, humans are erotic creatures – creatures that are oriented by love and passion and desire.

Plato used the term "eros" – the inner desire and yearning of the human being for the true, the good, and the beautiful. This yearning passes by way of sexuality, but it points beyond it as well. *Eros* speaks to our longing for transcendence – for a beauty, for a love that is ultimately beyond what this world has to offer. Ironically, however, "*eros*" cannot be satisfied by the merely "erotic." The desire to satisfy these erotic feelings by the homosexuals is a misguided one. Even the great psychologist Freud understood this for he wrote: "with the possibility that something in the nature of the sexual instinct itself is unfavourable to the realisation of complete satisfaction" (*"On the Universal Tendency to Debasement in the Sphere of Love, sect.3.)*

And it is on this point that the homosexuals go wrong. Homosexuals are continually promised "complete satisfaction" which is a mere appeal to the "*eros*" and this is what I refer to as "bastardization of the erotic." To "bastardize" means to debase something – to reduce from a high state to a lower state. That's precisely what's happening today when we imagine that "*eros*" can be satisfied by same-sex relationships, prostitution and bestiality, to mention but a few. The union of man and woman – as beautiful and wonderful as it can be – is only a sign, an icon that is meant to point us to something infinitely greater – the love of God Himself! As Augustine famously put it, "You have made us for yourself, oh God, and our hearts are restless until they rest in you."

Monsignor Lorenzo Albacete, put it this way: "We talk about different 'sexual orientations' in human life. But the ultimate orientation of human sexuality is the human heart's yearning for infinity. Human sexuality, therefore, is a sign of eternity." This means that the "erotic – even misdirected eros – is a sign of the kinds of animals we are: creatures who *desire* God.

Christians are right to raise serious concerns about the provocative nature of certain sexual orientations. But how should we respond? Rather than condemning the homosexuals outright, Christians should honour what the homosexuals have got right – that we are creatures of desire – and then responded *in kind* with counter-measures that demonstrate where desire really points us – towards God!

Chapter Two

DIVORCE:
Going Against the Will of God

Defining Divorce

Divorce simply means the termination of marriage. It involves canceling the legal duties and responsibilities that two married people are supposed to share. Consequently, all the things that held the two people together: friendship, love, conjugality, children and many more fall apart.

As a matter of fact, the sexual embrace is the foundation stone of human life. The family and, in turn, human society itself springs from this embrace. Marriage and the family unit come to an end when the sexual relationship terminates. As marriage and the family go, so goes civilization. How ideological this must seem! Civilization ending with a sexual embrace in marriage! Rather far-fetched I guess. The evidence available demonstrates that the devastating physical, emotional and financial effects that divorce has on the children of broken marriages will last well into adulthood and may even affect future generations. This is where civilization starts being crippled. With such devastating effects on the future generation, how do we expect the world to advance? Before I go on to discuss all about Divorce and how it affects the world, I will first introduce the meaning of marriage.

The Meaning of Marriage

Marriage, according to Christopher West, a contemporary theologian, is the intimate, exclusive, indissoluble communion of life and love entered into by a man and woman at the design of the Creator for the purpose of their own good and for the procreation and education of children. Marriage is therefore the closest and most intimate of human friendships. It involves the sharing of the whole of one's life with his/her spouse. It calls for a mutual self-surrender – so intimate and complete that spouses, without losing their individuality, become "one" in body and in soul.

To call marriage an indissoluble communion of life and love is to say that husband and wife are not joined by a passing emotion or by mere erotic inclinations which, selfishly pursued, fade quickly away. They are joined in authentic conjugal love by the firm and irrevocable act of their own will. Once their mutual consent has been consummated through genital intercourse, an unbreakable bond is established between the spouses.

There is such widespread confusion today about the nature of marriage that some would wish to extend a legal "right" to people who intend to come out of it. The very nature of marriage makes such a proposition impossible. While marriage involves a legal contract, this must be subordinate to the spousal covenant which provides a stronger and more sacred framework for marriage. A covenant goes beyond the minimum rights and responsibilities guaranteed by a contract. A covenant calls the spouses to share in the free, total, faithful, and fruitful love of God. It is God who, in the image of his own Covenant with his people, joins the spouses in a more binding and sacred way than any human contract. To do the opposite is to rapture, to desecrate the core of family life which is the pivot for love, unity leading to a better world. In today's world where divorce has become almost a pandemic, there is cause for alarm.

Among my naughty friends at one time were those who either had only had little or no contact with their parents. Their common characteristic was a Dutch father and a Ugandan mother living in London. In many cases, these children had never seen their father as he returned to his home country as soon as the mother conceived. Another category was that of children who could openly tell you that their parents actually separated when they were growing up. This had deeply affected them both socially and emotionally. Such children were very aggressive, always felt insecure and the found it difficult to adapt to a change in the environment. Even among their peers, it was often difficult for them to mix with the rest of their friends in school. Most of the children from such family backgrounds are faced with this negative impact. I observed that in order to get over the frustration of the separation of their parents, such children often got themselves into drinking, smoking and to a large extent other addictions. This is a mere tip of the iceberg. It just is a simple micro-cosmic projection of the devastation divorce can cause on the child and the nation at large.

Divorce and its Effects on Marriage

Today divorce seems to be a cure for all kinds of problems in a marriage. Couples with personal and business difficulties only see divorce as an easy solution since it is acceptable any way. In fact in the US some people go through divorce not because they must but because they consider it "trendy" and since everyone's doing it, they too should just follow along. These days, the constant image of celebrities marrying, divorcing and re-marrying at such a rapid rate in the American pop culture places the public in the mindset that marriage is entirely superficial, the popular thing to try out without commitment in any relationship.

Marriage has been marred and corrupted by today's culture, and is not regarded as it was before. For instance, at an average US high school, any child is as likely as not to have parents that are separated or divorced. Statistics show that as of 2002, 38% of marriages in the U.S. ended in divorce, not counting the divorces in California, Colorado, Indiana, and Louisiana which don't keep statistics on divorces.

In Uganda, where divorces used to be rarely heard of, today it is a thing many younger people advocate for, especially under the guise of human rights. It is not uncommon for the courts of law to be inundated with divorce cases. Being this widespread, its effects can be seen on family life, educational attainment, job stability, income potential, physical and emotional health, drug abuse and crime. It should also be noted that the effects of divorce on children and the nation can range from mild to severe and from short term to long term.

Divorce and Crime

The divorce of parents, however amicable, tears apart the family – the fundamental unit of society. It should not be a surprise that issues like crime are racing to top the charts in our societies. This is ultimately because of the strong relationship between family background and problems like crime. To be able to understand such a relationship, one must consider the evidence that is available.

In a British longitudinal study of males aged 8 to 32, David P. Farrington, Professor of Criminology at Cambridge University, found that the divorce of parents before a child reached age 10 is a major predictor of adolescent delinquency and adult criminality. In a study carried out in 1998, a U.S. longitudinal study which tracked over 6,400 boys over a period of 20 years (well into their adult years) found that children without biological fathers in the home are roughly three times more likely to commit a crime that leads to incarceration than are children from families that remain intact.

The above studies, though done far away from Uganda, are a proper reflection of the reality which is Universal and affects people in the same way. The studies also seem to agree with the grandfathers of psychology like Sigmund Freud who held that "the most common element that contributes to criminal behaviour is faulty identification by a child with her or his parents". In his view, the improperly socialized child as is in the case of a child brought up by a divorced couple "may develop a personality disturbance that causes her or him to direct antisocial impulses inward or outward. The child who directs them outward becomes a criminal."

This therefore means that the rise in the numbers of

delinquents in our societies and the rate at which crimes committed by children is rapidly shooting up are just concomitant with the rate of divorce. If nothing is done to curb the rate of divorce, we can imagine what our society might be like by the end of this century.

Divorce and Educational Achievement

In the words of former US president, John F. Kennedy: *"our progress as a nation can be no swifter than our progress in Education, the human mind is a fundamental resource"*. If there is anything that counter-attacks such a proposition, it is the negative effect of divorce on children and the nation at large. One of the dangers of divorce is its impediment of proper education to children of parents who get divorced. The main reason for this is clear. Children from such homes do not get the time required to concentrate on their studies. They are filled with anxiety caused by the separation and the incessant vacillations from father to mother and consequently they never have proper educational patterns. Imagine a child whose parents have divorced and the mother lives in London while the father is in Kampala as happens often. The only pleasure that such a child may enjoy are the long trips to and from London but they may never concentrate on their studies. Take into account that actually the study systems in London and Kampala might be fundamentally different. While the child may have been raised up in a purely local UNEB school such as Kitante High School in Kampala, he/she gets a challenge on arriving in London and they find that the GCE (General School Certificate) syllabus is completely different for that matter. In the long run, the poor child is left at the centre of the drama. Such children who are known for poor adaptability to the new environment end up becoming challenged and may even drop out of school. All this happens as a result of the decision of the parents to divorce. In addition to the above, even when children from divorce families persist with education, they are less likely to graduate as compared to those from the secure families.

Judith Wallerstein, a clinical psychologist from San Francisco, found that of the college-age students who went to the same high schools in affluent Marin County near San Francisco, only two thirds of children from divorced families attended college compared to 85 percent of students from secure families. Such statistics well illustrate this point. Can civilization be attained through poor performance, failure to achieve full education all because of the "nomadism" caused by divorce?

Divorce and Family Income

Post-divorce families usually suffer financially. In fact evidence shows that this economic effect is more negative to families than the great economic depression was to America as a nation. That is to say that the rate of financial recession caused to the family due to divorce is above the 30% mark of the 1929-1933 economic depression. Studies show that women experiencing divorce face roughly over 30 percent decline in the standard of living they enjoyed while married and men show a 10 percent decline. The consistency of this finding caused one researcher to conclude: *"However 'prepared' for marital disruption women increasingly may be, they are not prepared in ways sufficient to cushion the economic cost."*

The divorce itself can be a financial hurdle. While some divorce proceedings are relatively inexpensive, the fees can soar. Specialists say the legal fees involved usually vary according to the case. Attorney John Crouch describes it this way: "You can get a divorce for under $10,000 per spouse in lawyer fees if you're lucky and if both the spouses and their lawyers are reasonable and fair. This does not include what the divorce does to the standard of living, or having to pay child support, or the expenses of visitation. But you really can't predict even that. ... Either side can pull all kinds of stuff in court that just makes both the lawyers waste time until one client runs out of money. I just finished one case where they settled, but then the husband had to spend $70,000 just to enforce the settlement agreement!"

Divorce may not cost that much in Uganda but we are heading that way sure enough! This example may be foreign to many but if you are reading this, you surely have the opportunity to look at today's currency rates and make a conversion. The point to make is not in the pounds or shillings the legal proceedings may cost. It is that such expenses usually leave one party faced with inability to cater for their financial needs. This automatically puts the children of such a couple in a tight corner with no financial caretaker to adequately provide for them. The irony is that while married couples are supposed to build business empires, ensure financial freedom for their children, divorcing couples only tear down all that they worked hard at in a matter of hours.

Divorce and Sex Orientation

Many young people from divorced families struggle with feelings of inadequacy and frequently turn these feelings into erroneous judgments of peer rejection. Daughters of divorce find it more difficult to value their femininity or to believe that they are genuinely lovable. And consequently this affects not only their love life but also their entire social life. Sons of divorced parents too frequently demonstrate less confidence in their ability to relate with women both at work and romantically. In extreme cases, these children end up with disordered desires that if not controlled may result in same-sex attractions in form of homosexuality or even bestiality (attraction to animals). In mild cases, however, such children are affected with unrest in relationships. They tend to move from one relationship to another without realizing the "sores" they inflict upon themselves and on their multiple "partners". Through the mirror of the failed love relationship between their parents, they too consider love a hide-and-seek kind of affair that never deserves commitment. There is common talk among many teenagers today that single parenthood is the way to go. All these can be traced back to phenomena like divorce.

In all this madness, however, all hope is not gone. Children, especially pre-teen children (ages 9 to 12), who maintain a good relationship and frequent contact with their fathers after a divorce are better able to maintain their self-confidence. Staying glued to their mothers alone after divorce can be very detrimental, especially for boys. It is therefore important that even after divorce, both parents should share responsibility in the upbringing of the children to avert such abnormalities.

Divorce and Addiction

Today in Uganda and all around the world we are plagued with the highest levels of drug and substance abuse. What is appalling is that this kind of behaviour is even being exhibited by the youth and especially those in schools. I wonder whether those responsible for such children do take time to discover the real causes of these habits. Research shows that Children who use drugs and abuse alcohol are more likely to come from family backgrounds characterized by parental conflict and parental rejection. Divorce increases these factors, and hence increases the likelihood that children will abuse alcohol and begin using drugs. Adolescents whose parents recently divorced are found to abuse drugs and alcohol much more often than those adolescents whose parents divorced during their early childhood. When they are compared with children whose parents are still married, the difference grows even greater. Comparing all family structures, drug use in children is lowest in the married family that is intact.

Divorce and Health

It is very clear that divorce affects the health of children in broken families in many ways. The biggest of these health maladies is psychological, i.e. behavioural, emotional, and psychiatric. For instance, upon the break up of their families through divorce, children experience reactions ranging from anger, fear, and sadness to yearning, worry, rejection, conflicting loyalties, lowered self-confidence, heightened anxiety, loneliness and depression. In fact the health consequences of divorce are so severe that a Yale researcher concluded that being divorced and a non-smoker is only slightly less dangerous than smoking a pack a day and staying married. Such adverse effects are the leading causes of other health complications like hypertension and cancer. It is important to note that while both men and women suffer the psychological health illnesses, researchers have found that women are more greatly affected by these illnesses. They insist that women are more likely to be depressed, hostile, and have poor relations with other people.

Researchers from the John Hopkins University and the University of Chicago also found out that the children of divorced parents experience mental health problems significantly more often than the children of intact families. This is a big threat to the future of our societies and nations.

Owing to the divorce of their parents, many children are often victims of suicide. This is habitually triggered off by the children's negative thoughts. They think that the parents have rejected them and no longer have any interest in them. Such reality-based perceptions often become unbearable and the child ends up committing suicide. The more the divorce rates go up, the higher the suicide incidences registered will be.

Divorce does not only influence the psychological health of individuals, it also affects the physical health of those in its way. And when it does, it wreaks a lot of havoc. For instance, after a diagnosis of cancer, it has been found that married people are most likely to recover while the divorced are least likely to do so. The reason behind such a finding is clear: the emotional trauma caused by divorce has serious negative impacts on the physical health of the body.

Conclusion

It is true that while a marriage begins and still ends with the two parties (man and woman) involved, there are other stakeholders who must assert their position in order to save this precious institution. These are: the church, the family members on both sides of the couple (relatives) and the state.

- The church has made its stand clear that it can never be party to any divorce proceedings and this is encouraging. Still a lot more has to be done in the pre-marital counselling sessions which in most cases are rather shallow.
- The relatives of the couple intending to divorce should do whatever is within their ability to save the marriage. In any case they are in time going to be hit by the after-shocks of the divorce. Their indifference in the face of divorce, coupled with their encouragement of the proceedings, should never be condoned.
- The state should find means of making divorce inaccessible.

Chapter Three

DRUG ABUSE:
Reversing Healing Power

The concept usually referred to as 'drug abuse' is mainly constructed along moralist grounds. It tries to depict a situation whereby a drug that has primarily been created or manufactured to have a positive impact on a human being and his/her life and health is used wrongly and hence leading to negative results. Drug abuse is a social problem that is currently affecting both the developed and developing worlds alike, and is tending to cut across all ages, though, with a greater concentration amongst the youths.

First and foremost, a 'drug' is defined as any substance that produces a therapeutic or non-therapeutic effect in the body. Therapy ideally refers to curing. A drug is therefore essentially supposed to be taken for the curing/therapeutic effect on the consumer. Therefore, drug abuse refers to the situation whereby this primary reason for drug taking is not considered before or during the consumption of the drugs. For the person participating in drug abuse, the primary reason of curing the body of an ailment does not exist. The taking of the drug is then a sort of wilful "entertainment" for the "high" feeling that it gives the consumer.

Various reasons have been fronted as to what drives people into the habit and situation of drug abuse. It is important that we understand beforehand that drug abuse has different levels, phases and faces. Some drug abusers have sporadic treats, others engage in it permanently, and others, in addition to taking drugs, also engage in the trade of the same. Various reasons can explain this.

Drug abuse and its causes was first conceptualized by Rhodes and Jason (1988).It was later modified to create the modified Social Stress Model which incorporates environmental, social and cultural variables which impact drug abuse and also acknowledges the role of physical properties of the drug used and its interaction with the user.

(Dis)Stress

Stress and distress are major factors that drive people towards drug abuse. Major events in life like the death of a parent, abandonment, natural disasters and personal injury, which more often than not occur suddenly and without warning, leave the adolescent or any other individual without any control over the situation. This can result in that individual resorting to taking drugs to help cope with the pain or to assist in the period of adjustment.

Drugs are also taken to help one endure life's strains over adequate food, clothing, money and access to employment and recreation. These are the causes for the children who stay in 'ghettos' to get drawn into participating in drug abuse. It is the only way for people like that to survive in an otherwise bleak environment.

Life transitions also contribute to drug taking. When an adolescent moves from one society to another, or from one city to another, he or she may be forced to take drugs to gain acceptance in the new society he or she has moved into. Developmental changes may also be a challenge to an adolescent, or any other individual. As a person grows, he or she may be faced with changes that include taking care of their parents and siblings, due to factors like sickness of the parents, death of a parent or imprisonment. Others need to adapt to the challenges of a parenting role due to teenage pregnancy. These people end up using drugs as an attempt to cope with their lives and stresses.

Also, infectious diseases and malnourishment, common among street children, may result in retardation of growth, delayed puberty, skin diseases and bone deformity. These problems can greatly affect self-image and esteem, thereby driving the individual into drug taking as a way of seeking alternative self-recognition and actualization.

Normalisation of Drug Use

The concept 'Normalization' derives from the adjective 'normal', which contextually refers to those systems and sub-systems: environmental, social and cultural factors which have been shown to, or considered likely to contribute to or influence drug use. These may include the following:

(a) The price of the drug: This determines who and who will not access it. This is because the financial cost tagged to a drug will certainly prohibit those who cannot afford it from accessing it. The cheaper the drug, the more its demand will be. That is why cheap drugs like glue, solvents and petrol are more widely used than other drugs like cocaine.

(b) The availability of the drug also determines or influences drug abuse levels in a society. For the legally accepted drugs, society determines their usage on both quality and quantity. For the illicit ones, measures are put to stop their availability in society.

(c) The capacity of the state or any responsible organ that is in charge of checking drug availability will determine the proportion of people who can participate in drug abuse in that specific society.

(d) Advertising and sponsorship has also contributed much to drug abuse in most societies. In most societies where adolescents lack hero figures and attractive models in their communities, attractive adverts of cigarettes and alcohol often lure them into drug abuse. Moreover, the showing of acts of smoking, boozing and drug abuse like cocaine in movies or television often makes it attractive to youths who want to be like the stereotype heroes and stars they watch on screen.

Drug Effect/Experience

It is important to note that different drugs produce different effects on the human body. It is also important to understand that the background of the person taking the drug is 'to feel the difference'. The person taking the drug is possibly trying to run away from misery, stress or burden into the state that he or she desires. Therefore, the effect of a particular drug on the body will determine whether he or she should continue taking the same. In most cases, wherever there is any altered mood or state of change in consciousness, this will act as a gateway into the world of drug taking.

Attachments

Different individuals have different attachments to different social groups. An individual can never have the same attachment to the family as to the school or workplace, and as to the peer group. A number of factors may determine the levels of attachment to a group that include a person's exposure to opportunities and influence within the group. A person who has strong positive attachment to the family or other social group is less likely to develop attachments to drug using peer groups that use drugs in a harmful or dysfunctional manner. It is the lack of attachment to a specific positive social group that drives an individual into joining drug taking groups so as to get a sense of belonging and social attachment.

Coping Strategies and Skills

In childhood and adolescence, various skills are acquired. These skills help an individual to solve life's problems and stresses. To cope effectively, an individual require large amounts of coping and social skills if he or she is to remain afloat in life. Rhodes and Jason (1988) identify two categories of skills: cognitive and behavioural. Cognitive skills include self-assurance, cognitive restructuring, cognitive distraction and self control. Behavioural skills on the other hand include problem solving, direct action through negotiation or compromise, withdrawal through leaving or avoiding the situation, communication skills, assertiveness, social networking, engaging in alternative activities and relationships. A person who is well endowed with these skills cannot easily move into drug abuse, since these skills provide him or her with the skills necessary for solving life's problems, stresses and challenges.

Resources

The availability of and access to resources has got a strong effect on the individual. It is mainly as a result of stressors that are usually a result of need that lead people into drug abuse. Therefore, access to health, educational, vocational, and recreational services has the potential to impact on one's choice on drug abuse since it eliminates the stressor that acts as the primary cause of the problem. An individual who is sick and feeling pain but does not have the resources to acquire heath resources decides to move into drug abuse so as to 'forget' the problem. The same applies to someone who needs to go to school but does not have the fees required, or someone interested in recreational activities but cannot afford to access them. Recourse to drugs is usually 'a coping strategy' for the un-resourced and under-resourced to cater for the stress of inability to access their need.

Therefore, from the above illustration contained in the Social Stress Model, the causes of drug taking can be said to include boredom, curiosity and the need to feel good, to relieve hunger and/or adopt a rebellious stance, to keep awake or get to sleep, early sexual activity, crime, educational failure, family disintegration, poverty, lack of accessible and useful recreational activities, lack of suitable alternative accommodation if the child cannot stay at home, relocation, oppression and discrimination availability of drugs and pressure from drug dealers, among others.

Drugs are taken in different forms and these include alcohol, tobacco, prescribed medication that is abused, inhalants, over-the-counter cough, cold, sleep and diet medications whose dosage is abused to create excitement in the person, marijuana, stimulants, club drugs that are taken by youths in night clubs, depressants that are normally used medically to relieve anxiety, irritability and tension, heroin and lastly steroids that are related to the male sex hormone testosterone.

There are many effects of drug abuse and they can be grouped as physical and emotional.

Physically, fighting and engaging in unprotected sex is a common result of involvement in drug abuse. This is because the drugs alter the normal thinking of the human being and leave him/her with no self-control.

Also, there are various health-related problems that go

with drug taking, depending on the drug used. These are mainly respiratory problems and brain damage, mainly because these are the body parts through which drugs are introduced to the body and meant to affect, respectively.

Malnutrition is also another effect that comes up mainly because the drugs suppress appetite or in some cases, due to lack of resources, the individual diverts money for food into drug acquisition.

In the most dangerous circumstances, there are dangerous health effects on the sexuality of the person mainly as a result of the use of steroids.

For the man, there is a shrinking of the testicles, reduced sperm count, impotence, baldness, difficulty or pain in urinating, development of breasts and enlarged prostate.

For the woman, there is masculinisation (clitoris enlargement, facial hair, cessation of the menstrual cycle, deepened voice and breast reduction.

In both sexes, it may lead to dangerous health effects like acne, trembling, swelling of feet and ankles, bad breath, high blood pressure, liver damage and cancers. Aching joints, increased chance of injury to tendons, ligaments and muscles are also a result of persistent drug taking. Emotionally, drug abusers have tendencies of developing dependence on the drugs, violence and aggression. There is development of poor judgement which endangers the life of the drug taker. Personality change and sudden mood changes are also common with drug abusers.

Drug substance abuse also has strong social impacts. It is said to be the number one reason for rampant child abuse in the United States of America. A family that has either or both parents involved in drug abuse is more susceptible to break down. Also a family that has a child involved in drug abuse more often than not faces family breakdown. The issue to consider therefore is what should be done to avert this state of affairs.

First and foremost, it is important to note that for drug abuse to exist and flourish there must be some structural deficiencies that make it possible. These may be political, economic and social and for drug abuse to be solved, these deficiencies must first be addressed.

Politically, the need for strong policies and legislation against drug abuse is important. This should be coupled with strong and capable systems and agencies to counter the social evil.

Moreover, domestic violence has been partly blamed on drug abuse. Police reports indicate that probably 50% of the people arrested blame alcohol for the hazardous acts committed in families.

Economically, the need to empower the poor in society is paramount. As a result of the realization that some people get involved in drug abuse to counter the stress accrued from lack of resources, the need to empower individuals and societies to access resources is paramount if drug abuse is to be contained.

Socially, there is a need to create a strong and cohesive social structure if drug abuse is to be checked. Drug abuse accrues from the failure of society to offer attachment and hope to an individual. This should first be within the institution of the family, and then be introduced to other social groupings that individuals belong to. A culture that is against the abuse of drugs is also paramount if the evil is to be checked. This breaks the 'normalization' of the social evil. This can be done through campaigns against or stipulating the dangers of drug abuse.

In conclusion, drug abuse has multi-pronged causes and occurs in different forms, and therefore for it to be addressed, the various issues that cause it and the various modes in which it exists need to be addressed for the social problem to be addressed.

Chapter Four

PROSTITUTION:
Love for Sale

Prostitution is a practice of engaging (indulging) in promiscuous sexual relations, especially for payment in cash or kind. Payments in the form of money or goods depend on the complexity of the local economic system.

People who provide sexual accessibility on payment are called sexual workers or prostitutes.

Despite of all the moral and legal condemnation, prostitution is increasing rapidly in the whole world, to the extent that some countries have introduced laws to try and curb the practice. For example, in Netherlands, laws were not condemning prostitution as an act but it was an offence to profit from the earnings of a prostitute. This was according to the Brothel Prohibition Act of 1911. In 1996, a new legislation was adopted to condemn criminalization of Brothels. Instead, regulation was made in form of licensing Brothels, the number of prostitutes in the Brothels and the type of commercial sex they could engage in.

According to the Uganda Penal Code Section 134(A), a prostitute is "any person who either in public or elsewhere regularly or habitually holds himself or herself as available for sexual intercourse for money or other material gains."

The clients of prostitutes use them for a variety of reasons. For many of men, the motive is often to practice what they read in novels and watch in blue movies. This leads to sexual expression without controls on behaviour.

Background

Prostitution is very old, and determining its origin is hard. In the ancient Middle East, it was related to religious rituals in the temples of the fertility gods and goddesses of Babylonians. Women affiliated with the temple performance sexual intercourse with strangers who visited the temple to honour fertility and the sexual power of the goddess. Customary rewards were in form of donations to the temple, and those women would have access to land, slaves and social prestige.

In East Asian societies, such as Japan, China and Vietnam, there were women who provided services which include cultural aspects like music, poetry, dance and sexual services to men of the serving aristocracy. These women were recruited form all classes and were socially respected as artists and they had social influence depending on the men with whom they affiliated.

In Africa, prostitution was unheard of before the coming of the white man who changed the social, cultural, economic and political status of Africans. It is true, some African societies like the Kikuyu in Kenya had a tradition of offering their wives to visitors as a form of hospitality but this was not for exchange with anything. They did this because they agreed that the male sex drive is strong. They believed that men need a lot of sex and a variety of sexual partners and faithfulness is a woman's practice. The Bahima and Banyankole in Western Uganda believed that a woman belonged to a clan not to one man and the father-in-law was the first to sleep with the newly wedded woman. Africans did all these as cultural norms which created unity and respect.

In African traditions, one husband would have as many wives as he could manage. However, in prostitution, it is not marriage. It is a monetary transaction where the seller, commodity and market place are the human body.

Today, men do not want to have many wives because that would mean a whole lot of responsibility. They instead prefer, having one wife, and in situations when she can not satisfy their sexual desires they 'buy' prostitutes to do it.

Prostitution in East Africa began with the flourishing of small towns and the booming trade in inland towns that led to the creation of urban communities that lived outside the norms of society. The men and women this trade attracted were mostly unmarried. The women ended up in prostitution because there were few regular jobs for them whereas the young men did not have enough money to marry.

The form of prostitution they engaged in was either *watembezi* or *wazi wazi*. The *watembezi* prostitutes worked the streets, soliciting customers who passed by. *Wazi wazi* prostitution originated from Tanganyika and Uganda women who wanted quick profits but feared the possibility of arrest and deportation.

One Tooro woman who went to Pumwani in 1946 was quoted as saying: "Because I was poor in Uganda, I engaged in day time *watembezi* prostitution and welcomed everyman. I had no money so I had to go with every customer who could not afford to choose one tribe over another, but other Uganda women, particularly those who lived in Nairobi for a few years, sought out those groups of men who would pay them the most."

Prostitution is of two types. One is contractual prostitution. Here, a man and a woman enter into a contract and agree on the payment for the service to be offered. However, this contract is not like a capitalist one. The man and woman don't need to be capitalists. Patman asserts that the prostitute is exploited; whether he/she is taken as a worker or a petty entrepreneur because labour power is assumed to be contracted, not bought.

Trafficking of human cargo is believed to be the major cause of prostitution internationally. This involves not only men and women but also under-aged children who either pay for their passage or are coerced into services like providing cheap labour at near-slave rates of prostitution over which they have no control. It is believed that certain syndicates are involved in this for profit since they control the workers and their earnings.

Opponents of this form of this form of prostitution advocate what is known as the "abolitionist" approach, which declares that prostitution constitutes a violation of human rights and it is thus a form of human slavery. It therefore requires governments to abolish it through the penalization of "third party" beneficiaries from the proceeds of prostitution. They believe that without third party involvement, prostitution would wither away.

Katheleen Bany reveals that sexual slavery which happens when the prostitute is bought is actually taking place. Some girls are being sold in the guise of employment only to find themselves under the control of masters and whatever they earn ends up in the hands of their masters.

Emmanuel Kant also observed that sexual love makes the loved person an object of appetite. As soon as the appetite has been stilled, the person is cast aside as one casts away a fruit which has been sucked dry .Women engaged in any form of prostitution are not loved but are the subject of lust and gratification of men's sexual appetite. This degrades human nature. Thus prostitution is morally wrong since it subordinates the woman and makes her an object of sexual gratification.

In Uganda, prostitution is on the increase to the extent that even school girls who are provided with everything by their parents or guardians practice it to get more goodies from "sugar daddies" than their parents can offer.

The origin of prostitution in Uganda is hard to trace. It is thus based on theories and speculation. Like any other African country, the tradition allowed men to have sexual intercourse with unmarried women or widows. This was interpreted by the theorists as a coexistence with monogamous marriage. In African tradition, when a man died, his brother would take over his responsibilities as a man, which included having sexual intercourse with the widow in exchange for his protection. This led to polygamous co-existence to save the woman from becoming a victim to prostitution to meet her material and emotional needs.

Many schools of the thought have asserted that the origin of prostitution is East Africa was the World War II veterans who introduced the system of paying for sex which they had learnt overseas. Indian workers who were building the Uganda Railway fuelled the act by buying local women to have sex with. Another origin of prostitution that has been noted was the deportation of sex workers from Dubai in the early 90's because of their involvement in sex trade there. These women formed the biggest group of prostitutes and were popular among Arab expatriates in Kampala and other towns because of their unique sexual prowess commonly known as "Ugandan style".

The laws of Uganda condemn prostitution; not like in England, Netherlands, Wales, Ghana and other countries which compromise the issue.

Laws that were passed in 1941, before the Penal Code was drafted, condemned prostitution. In Buganda, for example, a woman was not supposed to act as a prostitute. Also, unmarried girls below the age of twenty would be committing an offense if they engaged in activities that took them a way from home at night. In Bukedi, similar laws were enacted/passed (laws of the protectorate).

However, these laws were not successful for they did not make any impact on the rise of prostitution. What this law did was to limit liberty of women but it did not stop prostitution.

However, it should be noted that laws of prostitution did not exist in pre-colonial Uganda. This is because cultural practices like widow-inheritance formed part of people's customs and were not regarded as offences. The only offences penalised were adultery, rape, incest, and bestiality.

Although prostitution is illegal in Uganda, no woman has been convicted of the offence of practicing or being engaged in prostitution. Moreover, it is almost impossible to prove that one is guilty of prostitution. This explains why girls are often rounded up by the police and only charged with being idle and disorderly.

Most of these prostitutes are found in bars, hotels and night clubs. They advertise themselves by being dressed in very short and tight clothes. Their time of operation is 9:00pm; they will enter a bar, sit at a specific place and begin drinking beers as they wait for clients to approach them. Others wait in street corners for any cars that pass by with a man inside. If it slows down, they follow it and start negotiations. They are then driven away if a deal is struck. Most of these girls are aged 16-23 years.

There are many causes of prostitution ranging from economic, social and political reasons. The situations and circumstances surrounding an individual in the society at a particular time are more influential in this case.

Economic hardship is the major cause of prostitution in Uganda and the world as a whole. In African tradition, there was nothing like lack of basic needs of life. It was the role of every member of the society to ensure that everyone accesses basic needs. However, with the coming of the white man, individualism increased. One had to work for his/her own increasing needs. Many girls therefore are pushed into prostitution because they lack basic needs of life and need to survive. This is common with women from a village background, daily wage earners and labourers. The little money they earn cannot sustain them and their families.

Broken families have also caused many girls and women to join prostitution. Broken families are caused by death or divorce. When the family head dies or drops his family for another woman, the woman has to use all means to sustain her family. Because jobs are not easily got, they find themselves practicing prostitution in order to provide for their children. Young girls who are left behind by their mother are cruelly treated by their step-mothers and they subsequently run a way to towns to find themselves jobs. These often end up as house-girls or prostitutes when they fail to find jobs. Those whose mothers are struggling to sustain them join prostitution to supplement what their mothers earn.

Childhood or teenage experience include sexual exploitation such as rape, seduction, or having been deceived and sold to a house of prostitution. This is done without their suspicion or by deceiving them that they will be given jobs in the city. After being deceived and lured into this act, they become helpless and feel stained and decide to do it full-time to survive. This is grilled into them as their only way of survival.

This was the experience of Pam (not her real name): "I was clothed in nice dresses, given good food and worked at Aunt Milly's home (not her true aunt) doing the house chores and selling in her shop at times. After a month of this good life, Aunt Milly said I was old enough to know the real source of her money. She took me to a house away from home where I was introduced to prostitution. At first I was appalled and I cried, but I have since known that it is my only means of survival"

Unemployment rate in Uganda is very high. According to the Uganda Bureau of Statistics, 3.3% of Ugandans are unemployed. 53% of these are females. Although women are unemployed, they have to sustain themselves. Most of them do not wish to leave towns and go back to villages to practice agriculture to survive. The youth have to be highly educated with experience because the employment opportunities are few. They will thus be dropped because they lack qualifications and some who are qualified lack "know-how". This increases the financial difficulties for most of them and they resort to this 'job' which does not need qualifications.

The tourist industry has also been marked as a source of employment, for tourists look at sexual pleasure as one of the attractions of Uganda and the prostitutes are eager to provide services in exchange for good money and nice goodies like the latest cell phones from abroad. They prefer to go with tourists even though they make unusual demands for sex such as oral sex. For example, Harriet (not her real name) is employed as a prostitute and her salary is 150,000/= per month. Her clients are whites and she keeps on changing them when they leave the country. She says: "African men do not know how to treat a woman; and that is why I go for white men." She does not receive direct payment from them; they pay her employer; but they offer her other gifts and pay her rent.

Poverty is the main cause for prostitution and all other causes originate from it. The poor migrate to towns for employment and good life because in their villages, agriculture is not found well to sustain their financial needs. There is no piped water and no electricity. This means that technical machines like computers and television cannot operate for those who can afford them. This encourages girls to come to towns to look for work and one of the forms of work where money is got quickly is prostitution. The present social and cultural conditions are facilitators of modern prostitution. Today, money has taken over virtues like goodness, honesty and sacrifice, as the sources of honour and respect which were important in African tradition. Consumer goods from foreign countries are more attractive and valued. They are a mark of power, honour and status. Thus, some girls who are materialistic have taken up prostitution in order to buy affluent goods, caring little about the degradation and violation of human dignity. One prostitute reveals that she earns 300,000/= per month and even people doing decent jobs borrow from her.

Demand for prostitutes is much and ready. Most men come to towns to look for jobs without their wives and some are not married. Some delay to marry because they lack money for traditional bride price and wedding parties. Others prefer to use prostitutes because there is no responsibility attached to them.

Other married men use prostitutes when their wives are not in a condition to offer sex, like when they are sick, pregnant or just tried. Some want to change partners or to practice the sex acts like oral sex which they watch in blue movies or read about in magazines and novels.

All these increase the demand for prostitutes and thus their supply also increases. There are some bars which welcome prostitutes who are meant to encourage customers to drink their beer.

Wars have also caused an increase of prostitution in Uganda which since independence has faced a lot of changes in government by *coup d'etat*. These wars leave most people in misery and helpless. They run away to towns for survival and end up in prostitution because they lack basic needs.

Western civilization is another cause of prostitution. The youth today are over-exposed to pornography such as blue movies, novels and magazines which arouse their sexual desires and they end up practicing prostitution without their knowledge.

Some girls are influenced by their mothers who are doing the same job. Others work with them in bars and encourage them to be good to clients so as to sell more. They thus end up in prostitution.

Prostitution has caused a lot of effects on the society. The number of street kids is increasing at a very high rate because prostitutes produce children whose fathers they don't know. Often these women run away from their children to another area of operation. Some children are dumped in garbage piles because their mothers do not want to be bothered with them. Others abort in order to get over the burden.

Prostitution has also reduced chances of unmarried men getting married because their sexual need is satisfied by prostitutes who make no other demands of them, so they have no responsibility.

Young girls who are introduced into prostitution look at marriage as not satisfying in terms of money and sex. They thus prefer the life of prostitution.

Prostitution is believed world wide to be a major cause of sexually transmitted diseases including HIV / Aids. In Ghana, public awareness campaigns on HIV/ Aids emphasise that sex workers are a source of HIV/ Aids. Seater associations in Ghana, which are composed of prostitutes who are home-based sex-workers, therefore in their information to members, they teach them about safe sex, and many carry condoms with them. However, the challenge they face is that some clients may refuse to use condoms and because they cannot stand to lose a client they are forced to have live sex.

Remedies

In addressing this social problem, the government has a big role to play. It is believed that not all these women like what they are doing but they are forced by economic hardships.

In a letter to the president by Peter Wankulu, a co-coordinator of the Organization of African Union (OAU) veterans, published in the *New Vision* newspaper of September 28th 2001, he says that prostitutes are forced into sex trade by the hard economic conditions in the country: "I doubt so highly whether so many women in Uganda would go public if they had other alternatives, and yet their economic situation is so difficult." The government therefore should set up income-generating activities for women who are unemployed; and also geared at helping former prostitutes to settle in the society.

The government should avail self-help loans to former prostitutes through micro-credit schemes hence reducing the percentage of unemployed women.

Most women are less educated than men because of cultural beliefs that provide education and property inheritance to the male child. To solve this social problem, the education system in the whole country should be availed to both sexes.

The economic system in the country should be adjusted so that job opportunities are increased and can be done by anybody that has been trained to do it, whether they have experience or not. Government should ensure implementation of just and equitable land distribution system so that the poor are able to access land and practice agriculture.

Former prostitutes should be given training on improved methods of agricultural production so that they can produce enough food for their needs and sell the surplus.

Those who refuse to adjust should be arrested and imprisoned. Uganda has been hard because the law presumes someone innocent until proved guilty. It is hard to prove one guilty of prostitution, since they do it in the dark and secretly.

The system of education in Uganda can also be earmarked to alleviate Uganda. It should be geared towards imparting vocational training. Thus, it will be producing job-creators not job-seekers.

In terms of development projects, the urban centres have been enjoying a lot of privileges. In villages, the roads are poor, there is no electricity, and the prices for their produce are poor. The government should therefore address these problems so that rural urban migration is no more.

Strong laws should be put in place to protect the poor and powerless from being exploited and introduced into prostitution.

Religious and cultural institutions should strengthen their efforts to attain moral and ethical standards of the society.

Counselling centres should be set up to help psychologically and emotionally affected prostitutes. They should use trained counsellors who can train reformed prostitutes to go and encourage their friends to reform too.

Chapter Five

WOMEN:
The Riskier Sex

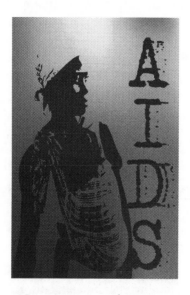

In this chapter I am arguing that women are more at risk of being infected with HIV than men because of social, economic and political inequalities that exist in a patriarchal society. I will argue that the unequal sex roles in the society enhance the level of HIV infection in women. I will discuss the society's attitudes and behaviour towards HIV/Aids victims. Furthermore I will discuss the reasons why there are higher rates of HIV/Aids occurrence in the developing countries than in Developed countries. I will point out the reasons why poor communities are more

HIV infected than rich communities. I will highlight how HIV is transmitted and suggest risk-reducing strategies.

HIV, according to nam publications (1996), is defined as the Human Immunodeficiency Virus. It is claimed that there are two types of HIV simply called HIV 1 and HIV 2. The latter is detected mainly in West Africa. It is suggested that HIV attacks the body's cells in the immune system (T4 cells) which normally play a vital role in preventing infection. In this way, the immune system is progressively weakened until completely destroyed (Powell, 1992).

AIDS is defined as Acquired Immune Deficiency Syndrome. This is a collection of specific illnesses and conditions which occur because the body's immune system has been damaged (Johnson et al, 1993, Berer, 1993).

It is claimed that HIV infection was first described in the medical literature in June, 1981, as a new and deadly disease that apparently affected only gay men and caused Aids (Weitz, 1991). But as Francome (1996) suggests, the HIV disease might have started as early as the late 1950s, but the media tended to shy away from it, until 1983 onwards when young children and those who received blood transfusion were affected by this disease.

For someone to be diagnosed as suffering from AIDS, he/she must have suffered at least one life- threatening, opportunistic infection or tumour. The opportunistic infections accepted under this definition of AIDS include: pneumocystis carini pneumonia (PCP), kaposi's sarcoma, fungal meningitis, Non-Hodgkin's lymphoma, severe chronic weight loss and encephalopathy (Youle et al 1988:117 -120).

The Joint United Nations Programme on HIV/AIDS (UNAIDS) and the World Health Organisation (WHO) released a shocking report to coincide with World Aids Day (1st December, 1997). This report reveals that 30.6 Million people were at the time believed to be living with HIV infection – one in every 100 sexually active adults worldwide – and that if the current transmission rates held steady, by the year 2000 the number of people living with HIV/AIDS would soar to 40 million! The total number of children under the age of 15 who were living with HIV/AIDS at the time was reported to be 1.1 million- this includes 590,000 new infections in 1997.

UNAIDS and WHO estimate that 5.8 million people were infected in 1997, at a rate of 16,000 new infections every day. UNAIDS report claims that because of lack of facilities for voluntary testing and counselling in the developing world, 9 out of 10 HIV infected people, had no idea they were infected. It is estimated that 2.3 million people died of AIDS in 1997- a 50% increase on 1996 - nearly half of those deaths were in women, and 460,000 were in children under 15.

The spread of HIV is primarily related to three means of transmission. Berer, (1993) suggested these to be: unprotected penetrative sex (anal or vaginal); injection of contaminated blood products (through transfusion or sharing of unclean injecting equipment); and maternal-foetal transmission (during pregnancy or childbirth).

During the early days of HIV disease, the public attitude towards HIV-infected persons was very negative. In the United Kingdom, HIV infection was seen as a mysterious gay cancer, and the "straight" people thought they were safe. Gay people on the other hand were apprehensive, seeing the response to the epidemic as a manipulated campaign to restrict their sexuality (Powell, 1992).

The social construction of HIV infection often characterises it as a deserved punishment for immoral behaviour. HIV infection is characterised by denial, condemnation, blame, prejudice, discrimination and stigmatisation by the individuals and society. These attitudes and beliefs significantly affect people with HIV, and drive them underground, making it difficult for Health authorities to control the epidemic (Powell, 1992).

Weitz (1993) reported that 71 per cent of the people interviewed in 1987 said that AIDS sufferers should be isolated from the rest of the society, arguing that AIDS was a punishment for the decline in moral standards, and therefore it was the people's fault if they got AIDS.

Triplet et al (1987) found that college students considered persons with HIV/AIDS responsible for their illness compared to persons with serum hepatitis, even though the latter is spread in the same way as HIV. Students would rather share a hospital room with a hepatitis patient rather than an HIV/AIDS patient, though hepatitis is considerably more infectious than HIV and can equally be deadly. Triplet further reports that students held homosexuals more responsible for the illness than heterosexuals. However, Garceau (1990) claimed that people who know someone with HIV are more likely to feel compassion for those most affected by AIDS.

Weitz (1991) clarified that people do not get HIV infection by sharing a room, being at school together, at work or socialising with someone who is HIV-infected. It is claimed that one must have sufficient amount of virus to be at risk. Weitz further claimed that fresh blood, semen, and vaginal cervical fluids contain enough of the virus for infection.

The pattern of spread which is emerging is one where heterosexual and maternal routes of transmission predominate. Francome (1996) claims that by 1993 many case of AIDS were attributed to heterosexual transmission in the United States of America. Kaleeba (1989) suggests that heterosexual transmission is mainly in developing countries – particularly in Africa – where polygamy is high. Kaleeba claims that many men in Uganda have more than one wife. She added that this is supported by the traditional attitudes which still prefer large families. The patriarchal society continues to define the primary function of a woman as childbearing. Therefore, a woman using a condom would be diverting from the norms of the society and would thus be considered 'abnormal' (Panos, 1990:17-18).

It is argued that if men have more sexual partners, then more women will be exposed to HIV by infected men than vice versa. This is fuelled by the fact that some religious organisations do not approve the use of condoms by women (*Monitor* newspaper, 2nd December, 1997).

Padian (1988) also claims that men appear to pass on HIV infection more efficiently than women during unprotected penetrative vaginal intercourse. This makes women more likely to be infected by men. Padian further claims that women get HIV infection at a younger age than men. This, he claims, is in line with socio-sexual norms.

It is argued that women tend to have sexual

relationships with men who are at least a few years older than them, whether inside or outside marriage (Johnson et al 1993). It is further claimed that married men often have extra-marital relations with younger women, in the hope that these women would be uninfected.

HIV infection through contaminated blood transfusion hits women disproportionately, particularly women in the poorest communities of developing countries. In 1990 WHO estimated that approximately 10 per cent of AIDS in sub-Sahara Africa had resulted from transfusion with infected blood (Chin, 1990). Berer further claimed that in Uganda, as many as 75 per cent of all adult blood transfusion was given to women who had faced severe bleeding in childbirth.

If a woman is not HIV infected, but comes in contact with a contaminated sperm (her partner's or from Artificial Insemination by donor), it is possible that she may be infected and consequently will infect her baby, Berer asserted.

Women feel depressed, angry and guilty when they discover that they have infected their newly born babies. Therefore, one of the most frequently asked questions by HIV-infected women is whether they will or will not transmit HIV to their babies.

Panos (1990:56-7) claims that there are two patterns of HIV progression in children who are infected by their mothers – either AIDS develops very early (within months rather than years) or the pattern is similar to that of adults, and children stay healthy for several years without showing signs of the HIV disease.

Laga (1990) claims that some Sexually Transmitted Diseases (STD's) such as gonorrhoea, chancroid, syphilis and genital herpes are associated with increased rates of HIV transmission, and are more easily transmitted from men to women.

However, Moreno (1989) pointed out that men, too, are at risk. Moreno claimed that 5 to 15 per cent of men are infected by female partners.

Drug abuse has been a prominent factor in the spread of HIV, primarily because intravenous drug users (IDUs) share injection equipment (Francome, 1996). The United States of America has the highest figure of intravenous drug users. Fullilove et al (1990) claim that a new form of cocaine called 'crack' introduced a new connection between drug use and HIV transmission. It is argued that the crack epidemic effects sexual behaviour and is responsible for the spread of Sexually Transmitted Diseases (STD's) including HIV infection. Fullilove claims that crack addicts will use whatever they have to obtain more crack. It is said that poor women will barter sex for drugs, and this sexual behaviour will facilitate transmission of disease to non-crack users.

Sterk et al (1990) argue that sex for drug exchange (SDE) is carried out for small sums of money in comparison with the established forms of prostitution. Sterk claimed that women feel powerless to resist requests to perform multiple oral and/or vaginal sex in order to obtain a small amount of crack. It is suggested that women were driven into this act by their desperate need for crack. One black woman who was interview by Sterk had this to say: "I sucked his dick, right, and he came in my mouth and I was spitting out, and he gave me $4. I was crying and shit because I knew how bad I (had) gotten. I was like, oh my god, $4 and I was out there beggin' for a fucking dollar"

(Sterk, 1990:60). That's how badly drug users may need the finances to support their habits.

HIV/AIDS in women is linked with other factors like minority status, social sex role, drug usage or poverty. The less bargaining power the woman has, the harder it is to avoid taking risks. The use of condoms has been recommended for safer sex, but a woman fears that if she insists on the condom being used, it might result in a violent assault on her or she might endanger her relationship or perhaps lose her partner. In this case, she will have lost someone who provides her with emotional contentment, social status and financial support. Therefore, for many women, fear of abandonment or violence ensures their compliance (Johnson et al, 1993:136-7). Squire (1993) argues that the women who have dependant children are even more vulnerable.

The UNAIDS/WHO report (1st December, 1997) has reported that drug injection is behind the dramatic surge in HIV infection in several Eastern nations, accounting for the majority of the 100,000 new infections which occurred in 1997, half of them being women. The report reveals that about 350,000 drug users in Russia share injecting equipment.

Squire (1993) argues that while black women in the USA account for 18 per cent of the total female population, they account for 74 per cent of the women with AIDS. Squire further points out that the level of HIV infection were 5 to 15 times higher among black women than among white women. Inequality and poverty are the underlying factors which help the spread of the HIV virus in the black communities in general, and among women in particular. Edwards (1989) points out that drug injection reflects the frustration and anger of the marginalised and impoverished population, seeking escape through mood-altering drugs. HIV/AIDS has affected all social classes, but not equally. The infection will continue to affect upper and middle class, but HIV is also a disease of poverty. As Edwards points out, poor and ethnic minority women are disproportionately affected among cases of HIV/AIDS in women in developed countries. In the USA the affected women and their partners are more likely to be poor, from an ethnic minority and from a drug using community.

Singer et al (1990) claims that HIV/AIDS infection was growing very fast in the black predominantly Caribbean community while AIDS cases in upper and middle classes was diminishing. This view has been confirmed by the United Nations programme report on HIV/AIDS. The report reveals that out of the 30.6 million people then thought to be HIV positive, a shocking two thirds were in Africa. The report further indicates that there is a growing gap between the developed countries and developing countries concerning not only the scale of the spread of HIV, but also the mortality rate from AIDS.

It is claimed that in North America, Western Europe, Australia and New Zealand, newly available antiretroviral drugs are reducing the speed at which HIV-infected people develop AIDS, while AIDS cases continue to rise in minority communities. There is increasing evidence of the spread of HIV infection among the poorer and less educated peoples of the world (WHO, 1997).

The poor communities find it hard to access the new drugs and have profited less from prevention efforts (UNAIDS p.4). Take the example of the African community in the United Kingdom. Although the statistical evidence shows that combination therapies (say, d4t +ddi) are saving lives, and that some drugs like AZT can prevent mother-to-child transmission, not many Africans can get access to these drugs (Foundation News, December, 1996).

There has been a decline in infection in industrialised countries in Europe and the United States, thanks to the new drugs that seem to control the virus. However, Dr. Piot, the Executive Director of UNAIDS, acknowledging the hope that had been gained from the new drugs, had this to say: "This is certainly good news, but not good news for everybody. A new combination drug therapy can only be a dream for most people." (Reuters, 28th November, 1996)

In the absence of a vaccine and sufficient resources to have the new drugs available to everybody, the only defence lies in educating the people to change their sexual behaviour. As Johnson (1993:238) suggests, the minimum requirements for behavioural change are that the individuals perceive themselves to be at risk. It is very important to educate people about the nature of the infection and how it is transmitted. Many people hold some myths, fears and prejudice about HIV/AIDS due to misinformation or lack of information.

As Moss et al (1995) suggest the Government should put more resources in the area of Health. This will enable Health workers to put up Prevention, education and counselling programmes aimed at achieving sexual behavioural change in individuals and society. Through these education programmes, targeted individuals and groups (like, prostitutes and drug users) would be taught how to avoid risks and encouraged to use condoms; taught to avoid contaminated body fluids (say in the mouth or the rectum and during menstruation); how to avoid use of unsterilized equipment and above all learn how to negotiate sexual relationship between sexual partners. Through these programmes, people would be encouraged to protect themselves by their own behaviour. (Panos, 1990:80-6)

Women should be empowered and involved in the planning of HIV/AIDS programmes of education, prevention and counselling. The governments should support and encourage Women forums in which women can exchange ideas and discuss sexuality, sex, HIV/AIDS and treatment. Women and minority groups should be free from segregation and discrimination in employment, schools and hospitals. Males and females should be liberated from their sexual roles so that sexual equality can be promoted. (Berer, 1993:328)

As Johnson, (1993:270-273) suggests, access to appropriate medical care, social services and health education is crucial for all women who may have been exposed to HIV infection, irrespective of economic or/ and social status.

Of late a female condom has been available. However, while a male condom can be found from almost everywhere (in clinics, petrol stations, hotels and even in toilets) for free, the new female condom is expensive - £16 per packet (nam publications, 1997). All types of condoms should be heavily subsidised or supplied free of charge to whoever wants them. Prostitutes can then attempt to practice protected safer sex as the only option for them (Weltz, 1991). The UN should subsidise the new anti-HIV drugs so that poor countries can afford them for their citizens who are HIV infected.

As pointed out by Sims et al (1995:150-2), community health workers should be trained in how to care for someone with HIV/AIDS; how to give emotional and spiritual support accompanied by thorough and compassionate counselling services.

Lastly, I am of the opinion that, while the above strategies are being implemented, people infected by HIV/AIDS should in turn respect the autonomy and health of other people and take measures to prevent the transmission of HIV/AIDS to others.

Chapter Six

HIV/AIDS IN UGANDA:
A Strategy as Simple as ABC

History

By the time you read this, I have a feeling that the history of HIV/AIDS in Uganda is as well known to you as the fact that NSSF is the only indigenous trillion Organization in Uganda! If you didn't know this, now you know! The only other trillion organizations in the country are Stanbic

Bank and Standard Chartered Bank, which have origins from other countries. Bravo NSSF!

However, just in case you are a visitor to this country, the history of the HIV epidemic can be traced back to the early 1980s when the first cases of the disease were reported, albeit with a lot of ignorance on what its real nature and mode of spreading was. Given the nature of Africans, everything that cannot be readily explained is attributed to the supernatural, and therefore, in the early periods of its spread, HIV/AIDS was preached in pulpits as a punishment from God to the sinners – mainly because it was killing people without any due explanation as to the symptoms, the way it was spread from person to person, and possible ways of prevention. The people in the pulpits were not alone in making the disease assume a divinity status. The witch doctors made a lot of money from the ignorance and spiritual nature of African society by claiming that the disease was actually witchcraft. It therefore required their services in as far as neutralizing the spread of the disease in a family with one infected person, since the argument was that the patient had been bewitched and the other fellow family members will follow suit unless they were given a 'neutralizing agents' to deter the witchcraft from sweeping the whole family. The modus operandi of administering the 'neutralizing agent' was through cutting the patient with a sharp object to remove some blood, which was then mixed with other herbs which anybody could get from the bushes, and then transferred to bodies of the uninfected family members! In the process, families were swept by the epidemic at an alarming rate.

It is interesting to note that in areas where belief in the

supernatural or divinities was highly prevalent, like the rural areas, the spread of HIV/AIDS and specifically in relation to the phenomenon of families being swept away was more prevalent.

Then came the period of widespread scientific breakthroughs and discoveries on the nature of the virus that causes AIDS and eventually the informed age of the disease where various forms of media and artists like Philly Bongoley Lutaaya got involved in sensitizing the population about the disease, and eventually the national and international efforts to fight the disease. As a result, everyone in the country, including kids in baby class, are aware of what HIV/AIDS is, how it spreads, and how to avoid it.

The Spread of HIV/Aids

Various ways have been said to be responsible for the spread of HIV – the virus that causes AIDS. These include, among others, heterosexual intercourse, blood transfusion involving infected blood, mother to child transmissions at birth, homosexual intercourse, and re-using syringes and other objects that have been in contact with infected blood. To summarize the ways in which HIV is spread, it is simpler to say that it is passed from one person to another when the infected blood of one person gets into contact with the uninfected blood of another individual.

Every virus in history – be it a virus for the human beings like influenza, to bird flu, to computer viruses – have a specific part of the system on which they capitalize, survive, and spread. The Human Immune Virus survives and moves in human blood. Therefore, it is wrong to assert that HIV is spread through sexual intercourse with a person with the virus without stating it categorically that it has to move from the blood stream of the infected person to that of the uninfected person. The male and female sexual organs have got concealed blood vessels which are protected by the exterior muscles. In the process of sexual intercourse, these muscles tear off as a result of the friction involved in the exercise, exposing the blood vessels of the two people to each other. Even when the blood flow is not visible to the two during or after the intercourse, tiny blood drops move from one person to the other through the sexual fluids and therefore it is hard to tell whether or not there was movement of blood in the exercise. As a result, blood moves from one person to the other. The situation is made more fertile if either or both the partners have sores on their sexual parts. This makes tearing off and eventually movement of blood from one person to another obvious. Therefore, to sum it up, there are two pre-conditions for the spread of HIV from one body to another. First, there has to be movement of blood from one person to another, and secondly, the blood of either party has to be infected with the virus. This explains why breastfeeding a baby for an HIV infected parent is allowed up to when the baby is three months, because it is assumed that the baby will have developed milk teeth which can bite the breast of the mother and hence lead to the movement of blood from the mother's breast to the fragile gums of the toddler whose blood vessels are exposed because the body has not yet developed enough muscle to cover the vessels.

The Interventions

Over time, various interventions have been put up by the Ugandan government and the international community in combating the epidemic. However, most times, the ABC Strategy has been used most by almost all the stakeholders in the fight against the spread of the disease.

The 'A' of ABC

This is used to refer to 'Abstinence', which can be explained as a state of self-discipline, self-denial and self-restraint against involvement in sexual intercourse. It therefore calls for a person's non-involvement in sexual activity. In simpler terms, it means that having found out that using a mobile phones is hazardous to our brain, we should restrain ourselves from using them, thereby not enjoying the pleasure of communicating with our friends and loved ones! This is the question: How many human beings can do that? By all standards, and by nature, human beings are rebellious pleasure-seekers. Telling a human being to abstain and hence avoid HIV/AIDS is the same thing as saying that we should not buy sodas because the sugars therein are harmful to our bodies. But I always see the item on many families' shopping lists on the festive days like Christmas and Idd. Are we saying that we are taking poison for a delicacy? The truth is; everything that gives pleasure to a human being, whether good or bad is hard to restrain from. This makes the proposition of abstinence as a way of fighting HIV/AIDS more of an idealistic solution, than a practical intervention. How many people are abstaining? Are you?

The 'B' of the ABC

This one stands for 'Being faithful'. It therefore calls to the faculty of the 'heart' – the value creator. Essentially, a human being is divided into three segments which have often been called the 3Hs: H1 is the Head, H2 is the Heart, and H3 is the Hand. The head represents everything to do with brain or mind and thought. It therefore calls on our sense of reasoning and thinking out things in the right order. The Heart is the social evaluator and handles issues to do with feelings and discernment between the good and the bad. It deals with values, norms and attitudes on the environment. It ranks some actions as good and others as bad. The Hand on the other hand represents the body or action. It is the implementer. It is the slave. Whatever comes out of the H1 and H2 is implemented by H3. As any slave would do, the body does not participate in making the decisions. It simply works on the decision that has been reached by the debate between the thinker and the evaluator. So, this is what faithfulness is. The brain says HIV /AIDS is killing people and I need to keep myself and the body alive. It then puts up the various ways of avoiding the virus, among others faithfulness. But the next day, the eyes see this pretty, unavoidable lady and the brain thinks and re-thinks about the issue of faithfulness! It then sends the issue to the heart – the social evaluator. The heart then evaluates the situation and gives its verdict on what the societal norms expect of you. Then the head re-thinks, but the girl might not be having the virus, why should I deprive myself of the pleasure? Now, whatever comes out of this debate and counter-argument between the brain and the social evaluator will eventually determine whether you – the body, gets involved with the lady in question. So, faithfulness is about being true to oneself which is a virtue and a social norm. But this is the question, how many human beings are faithful to themselves, before they go to being faithful to their families and spouses? Are you faithful to yourself? Are you faithful to your fiancée or husband/wife? Are you faithful to your employer? Are you faithful to your society or country? Faithfulness is another idealistic solution to the problem of HIV/AIDS. Human beings are by nature cheats. They always want to get what does not belong to them and they will do that even when they know it is against the rules and against the social values and norms of their community.

The 'C' of ABC

The 'C' is the most controversial of the ABC strategy! This is because various groups and individuals define it differently. Some groups define 'C' as castration! This is the proposition of mainly the women's movement that propose that men who are HIV positive and tend to rape women should be castrated, thereby solving the problem once and for all! Others define it as Circumcision. This is because they argue that recent research findings have got it that men who are circumcised are 50% less likely to get the virus from sexual activity, mainly because the foreskin being removed reduces on the cells that are likely to be a potential target of the HIV and also with the removing of the foreskin, the probability of wear and tear and hence bleeding is reduced. This has led to many governments, including that of Rwanda, including compulsory male circumcision in their strategies to prevent the spread of HIV/AIDS.

However, the third component of the 'C' is Condom use or Condomising as some people put it. This is the most popular of all the 'C' interventions. It calls for the use of the now popular condoms in various brands, types and sizes before penetrative sexual intercourse so as to curtail the movement of blood from one body to the other. I must say this is the only practical aspect of all the ABC Strategy. That notwithstanding, it also has its shortfalls.

To start with, the manufacturers of the condoms themselves agree that they are not 100% effective in HIV Prevention as they get out of their factories. Now just see how they are handled after they get out of the factory. It is well labelled-Keep in a cool dry place. That is not my definition of the truck they'll move in from the factory to the ship; spend weeks on water travelling from their Switzerland factory to Mombasa, travel for another week or more by truck form Mombasa to the National Drug Authority warehouse in Kampala, keep in there for weeks stuffed up, then move by truck to the district stores to be stuffed again God knows for how long before they are finally distributed to the retail shopper down in Isingiro district or wherever who will rough-handle it whatever way he likes before it gets to the end-used maybe six months down the road.

We also need to study the directions for use. The proponents for the use of the condom insist that it be correctly and continuously used. I hope I won't have to ask you if you are sure you know how to use the condom correctly. Truth is, most people know how to use the condom from the workshops where it is put on bananas or pieces of wood as a demonstration kit. But how many know how to remove it correctly from their covers, correctly place it on their genitals, correctly use it and correctly remove it, without risking the contact of a drop of blood or semen from the condom itself to the body of the second party? Given the nature of sexual activity and the nature of the emotions involved, who gives all due diligence to make sure that all the rules are followed?

Also, how many people use the condom continuously? Tales of people who use it on the first round of sex and forget on the second and third are not that uncommon. Similarly, tales of people who use them in the first month of relationship, and forget all about them thereafter 'because they have learnt to trust each other' are not uncommon either. So why are we lying to ourselves when we say we are protecting ourselves?

The Anti-thesis

I am proposing a new module to be used in the fight against the spread of HIV/AIDS. I hope it does not put me at loggerheads with Professors of Medicine. I propose HIV Testing. As simple as that! Where is the whole point in abstaining to avoid HIV, if you are not sure you do not have it already? Where is the whole point in claiming you are being faithful to your partner so that you do not bring AIDS into the home when you are not sure whether or not the disease has not got in already but you are operating on your ignorance of the fact? Where is the rationale in using condoms to avoid acquiring the virus, when you are not sure of your not having it already?

This is what I think. Once you are sure you do not have the virus, you have reason to abstain, so that you do not acquire it. Once you are sure you do not have the virus, you have reason to be faithful to your partner for the good of your family. Likewise, when you know you don't have the virus, then you will always use a condom to make sure that the virus does not get to you by stealth. When you have got a reason not to do something, then you have successfully handled your H1 – the faculty of thinking and reasoning. Once your thinking and reasoning are in tandem with your H2 – the social evaluator – the chances are your H3 – the body will be at peace and you will find it easier to make practical what otherwise seems idealistic. So, move to your next door Health Centre and join me in the fight against the killer by getting an HIV Test done. And when we have finally created an AIDS-free generation, please don't forget to include me in the Guinness book of records for the discovery of the 21st Century!

In God we trust!

Chapter Seven

RAPE AND DEFILEMENT:
Taking Liberties with Sex

Sexual abuse continues to represent the most rapidly growing reported violent crime the world faces. This occurs to both girls and boys, although cases of boys who have been raped have not been given enough attention. For example, *The Monitor* newspaper on 30 March 1997 published a story of a 16 year old boy in Kamuli who was charged with defilement for making his teacher pregnant. The teacher was portrayed as a victim because she was married.

According to Schnelder and Reuters (1997), South Africa reported the highest number of rape cases. In Uganda, hardly a day passes without a report on rape or defilement in the media. According to the study conducted by National Council of Women and Children, (1997), 75% of the girls are raped before the age of seventeen. According to Kabuye (1996); 20,000 and 30,000 people living in Kampala today have been subjected to some kind of sexual abuse.

The draft of social welfare policy (1994) estimated that in Uganda over one million children under the age of 12 today had been sexually abused. Lack of adequate protection encourages rape in the society. Amanyire et al

(1997) noted that trusted teachers and helpers have taken advantage of the situation and the environment to defile children. Kanina (1997) too points out that even the law enforcers and other responsible figures are involved in defiling children.

Aware of the risks of HIV infection, many men are now actively seeking out young women and girls who they deem to be uninfected. Barton and Wamai (1994) echo this, where they point out that the pattern of old men engaging in sex with young girls seem to have been exacerbated by the Aids scourge.

Reacting to the escalating rise in rape cases, the government of Uganda in 1990 passed a capital offense for sexual abuse. Unfortunately, sexual abuse is the inlay crime where the duty of proving innocence lies mainly with the victim and is probably one with the lowest rate of conviction.

The conviction is further watered down by the trauma of physical examination, interrogation and court appearances to which the victims are subjected.

Moore and Rosenthal (1995), Rosenthal and Seligman, (1984), note that victims experience symptoms of post-traumatic stress disorder (PTSD). PTSD includes persistent reliving of a traumatic event, distressing dreams, sleeplessness and difficulties in concentration. The victims experience depression, fear, anxiety and restlessness. For most of the girls, the memories of sexual victimization later emerge when the survivor is faced with difficulties in adulthood.

According to Daniluk & Haverkemp (1993), clinicians have coined the term "sexual abuse survivors' syndrome" to describe the PTSD-like symptoms that often accompany a history of sexual abuse.

Background

Throughout history, women, girls and children have been subjected to sexual abuse. Tomorrow and Smith (1995), for example, estimate that 20-45% of women in the US and Canada were sexually abused as children.

According to Kabanza and Nakyobe (1994), in Uganda women in their reproductive age and children form the most vulnerable group of sexual abuse and they account for 70% of the total population. From 1995-1997, *The Monitor* newspaper reported 80 cases of rape and defilement, while the register (1995-1997) revealed 298 cases of rape and defilement in Kampala alone.

In a media analysis on child abuse (1986-1996), out of 486 cases reported, 207 were of child abuse.

Sexual abuse involves many forms of unwanted and unwelcome sexual attention.

Sandler (1990) defined rape as forceful sexual intercourse and Giller, et al (1991) defined it as sexual activity without the consent of another person. Intercourse gained by force, threats or when the woman is stupefied or unconscious from drugs or drink or when the woman is mentally retarded is also rape.

Defilement is having sexual intercourse with a girl under the age of 18 years. It does not matter whether she consents or not, for under the law of Uganda a girl under the age of 18 is considered a child.

Causes of Rape

Whatever form sexual abuse takes, it is exploitation by an adult of the vulnerable situation of another person. This, according to Nyonyintono and Yiga (1994), includes ease of access, helplessness, ignorance of sexual matters and graft. Some parents have caused rape of young girls to increase by accepting to be bribed off so that they sit on the cases instead of pressing for prosecution. For example, *The Monitor* newspaper on 5th July 1997 and *Secrets* magazine issued on 24th July 1997, published the story of a girl who was raped by a local football star, Majid Musisi, and the case was settled out of court because her relatives preferred money to justice.

Violence of men against women, which is on the increase, is also another cause of rape. Defined as having sexual intercourse without the consent of the other person, rape means that women who are forced by their husbands to have sex are also being raped and their rights are being violated. It is a violation of the integrity of a person's body and also a violation of a basic human right to security of person.

Entrusting girls to people who are not their relatives has also increased the problem of rape and defilement. Many girls are not raped by strangers, but by their friends. According to a report by all African Press Service (1997), in the cases of girls who reported rape to police, 33%were raped by males in the neighbourhood, 9% by teachers, 3% by pastors and 3% each by brothers, fathers, and cousins.

Some girls invite rapists to themselves. They dress in very short skirts and stay out with boyfriends until late in the night. Some of them drink alcohol and when they get drunk, the same boys rape them. For example, *The New Vision* newspaper published an article on 29th October 1996, about three students from Lumumba Hall in Makerere University who were accused of raping a girl who was said to be drunk at that time. By dressing improperly and through their social behaviour, girls are blamed for inviting rape.

Women and girls in Uganda are disadvantaged groups. Their educational levels are too usually low compared to men's. This can be blamed on the African tradition where a boy child was believed to be more important, and in cases of economic hardships, the first priority would go to boys and girls would stay home preparing for marriage at an early age. Even when a boy raped a girl, the boy would be favoured and the girl blamed for seducing him. This has continued and has increased cases of rape because boys want to prove that they are real men.

Drug abuse is another cause of rape. Some men and boys rape children when they are under the influence of drugs.

Fear of HIV infection has also increased the cases of rape. Some men think that young girls are the only ones safe from HIV. They thus rape them so as to get satisfaction without acquiring the HIV virus.

Effects of Rape and Defilement

Rape has far-reaching effects on the child raped and her parents. The development of a child who lives in the midst of abusive situations such as sexual abuse is interrupted. According to Armsworth and Holaday (1993), it has been observed that trauma is particularly significant because of uncontrollable, terrifying experiences that may have their most profound effects when the central nervous system and cognitive functions have not yet fully matured. Even women who are raped suffer trauma. For example, in *The Monitor* newspaper of 27th August, 2003, there was a story of a woman who was raped by a man when she was giving birth, the experience that still traumatizes her whenever she is giving birth.

The predominance of anger, shame, guilt, fear, loneliness pain or any traumatic life experience in childhood are known to impair a child's emotional and cognitive development, ability to assimilate and process the trauma and subsequent life experiences.

It has been observed that immediately after rape, many victims experience feelings of humiliation, embarrassment, self-blame, revenge and guilt, fear of injury and death. There is sleep disturbance with inability to get sleep after sudden awakening, stomach or abdominal pains, genitor-urinary disturbances, headache or tension, loss of appetite and change in activity level to either lethargy or agitation.

Legal Ivory (1995), reveals that emotions after rape can be shock, disbelief and a feeling of being unclean.

According to Allers, et al (1992), and Baron et al (1997), women are likely to experience negative emotional reactions when sexually abused with immediate response of avoidance of and abstinence from sexual intimacy, which may lead to sexual dysfunctions such as reduction of sexual interest and pleasure, failure to get satisfaction during sexual activity and disturbing thoughts or feelings during sexual intercourse.

Many victims of rape are generally withdrawn from

involvement with other people. Moore and Rosenthal (1995), concur that rape victims compared to non-victims show low levels of self-esteem, a greater incidence of relationship problems, poor work satisfaction and less hope in the future for up to two years after the rape had occurred.

The victims of rape are likely to develop behavioural disorders including repetitive compulsive actions. To Carlson (1990), the people with obsessive-compulsive disorder suffer from obsessions, including thoughts that will not leave them and compulsive actions that they cannot keep from performing.

The feelings of hatred for sex may consequently, evoke aggression in victims whenever sexual activities are thought of. Some people tend to be self-destructive in that they exhibit a greater inclination toward suicidal behaviour, Benjack and Allers (1992).

Sexual abuse is closely associated with other problems or deviant behaviour. The victims are more likely to become chemically dependent to be involved in delinquent antisocial or criminal activities and to engage in prostitution and runaway behaviour.

To Carlson, et al (1988), whether a rape victim experiences serious psychological decomposition or not depends to a large extent on her past coping skills and on level of psychological functioning. The previously well-adjusted woman will regain her prior equilibrium, but rape can precipitate severe pathology in a woman with prior psychological difficulties.

Rape causes marriage break-ups because of sexual abnormalities that result from bad memories of the incident. Some victims fail to be sexually aroused, and thus any intercourse with their partners is like rape. This kind of sexual behaviour causes family break-ups.

In a research that was done on Luwero victims of rape by Bracken, Giller and Kalaganda, it was found that 75% of those raped were experiencing gynaecological problems like virginal discharge and pelvic pain. 66% no longer found sex enjoyable and 25% of the women developed negative feelings towards men.

Remedies

Sexual abuse is common and the psychosocial consequences suffered by the victims are well known. But there is very little attention being given to the victims in Uganda.

It is worth noting that often the rape/defilement victims significantly experience long lasting symptoms of posttraumatic stress disorder (PTSD) which disrupt victims' ability to function independently and engage in normal relationships. There has to be some remedy to this. Uganda is taking a firm position against defilement of children using the NGOs that have come up which centreed on the problems faced by children and women.

A campaign to change attitudes towards sexual abuse and welfare of victims is needed. A public stance should be taken by politicians, policy makers, media leaders and citizens to indicate that sexual abuse is socially unacceptable and contradicts societal emphasis on humane values, responsibility and respect for the rights of others.

A sexual education programme in schools, homes, and the community at large is needed. Counselling Centres that aim at promoting public consciousness and awareness to reduce sexual abuse are also required.

All medical practitioners, counsellors, law enforcers and the community at large should work hand in hand to provide alternative approaches, especially during physical examination, questioning and court appearances.

Community empowerment and self-determination programs are needed to address the issue of sexual abuse.

Victims and girls in general need to be reassured and encouraged that they are not helpless, powerless or unworthy. Self-determination and confidence will prevent and minimize sexual abuse.

Safe homes and neighbourhoods for children and families need to be created and maintained. The co-coordinated efforts of both communities and enforcement agencies are required to make neighbourhoods, schools and roads safe.

Education is needed for parents, educators, law enforcement workers and others. It should include strategies on conflict-resolution and alternative approaches to sexual abuse.

Parents should be their children's keepers, but not leaving them in the hands of teachers and houseboys who end up raping them.

Counselling should be offered to victims of rape to overcome trauma that results from such incidents.

Chapter Eight

REDUCING THE RATE OF RAPE:
Like It or Not, There Will Be Sex

In this chapter, I will first of all consider some different theories and statistics of rape, causes of rape, and lastly I will suggest the ways through which rates of rape can be reduced.

The law defines rape as a sexual intercourse with a female, who is not the wife of the perpetuator, which is accomplished without the consent of the female (Chappell et al 1977:66) By this definition, wives cannot be raped by their husbands, and neither can a man rape another man, nor woman rape another woman or man. Russell criticised this definition. She instead defines rape as intercourse imposed on a woman against her wishes, where her wishes are known to the rapist, or where she has expressed her wishes forthrightly, verbally, and/or physically (Russell, 1979:13)

Barbra Toner (1984) is of the view that rape is not merely a sexual act, but that it is a hostile act of aggression. Scully (1994:35) adds that rape is a neo-Freudian disease which is precipitated by the victim. Brownmiller in her book, *Against Our Will,* claims that rape is a conscious process of intimidation by which *all men* keep *all women* in a state of fear (Brownmiller, 1975:15).

It is not easy to know the prevalence of rape accurately, because just a small proportion of it is reported to police. The real figure might be five times higher than the official statistics (Francome, 1986:182). Rape is one of the most underreported crimes committed. Scully (1994) claims that between 25 per cent and 50 per cent of the cases of rape are unreported, and Holmes (1991:72) points out that habitual rapist, by the time they are caught, will have raped approximately fourteen times for each time they are caught. Holmes also argues that more than 50 per cent of all rapes occur in the home of the victim, and that 73 per cent of the time the rapist and the victim are of the same race (P73).

Scully (1994) claims that women are less likely to report rapes that involve men they know, and when they report an acquaintance of rape, they are less likely to be believed. Men in acquaintance-rape always deny that what they did was rape, and are less likely to be prosecuted, and if prosecuted they are less likely to be convicted.

As Bourque (1990:46) suggests, the police is insensitive to rape victims, and are suspicious of victims who had previously had willing sex with the rapist. Russell (1984:20) also claims that police treats rape victims as women who wanted to be raped, while Doctors perceive rape victims as prostitutes. Raped women do not say so when they visit their family doctors – for they cannot be believed. Young girls do not want to tell their parents of having been raped because they fear to be called whores. So they try to cope with it in their own way (Russell, 1984:24).

Francome (1990) suggests that one in five rapes is reported in Britain, while in USA it is one in eight. The official figures give underestimates of the actual number of rapes reported.

The under-reporting of rapes is blamed on the attitude of police and the judiciary towards women. As Scully argues, the police are very critical of rape victims, and it is the reason why women do not report rape because they are aware of the unfair treatment they are likely to receive from police and prosecutors.

Scully further suggests that women are more likely to report rape if it is of the classic kind – where a stranger invades a woman's home, attacks her in a public place, uses a dangerous weapon, or where the rapist physically injures the victim (Scully, 1991:6). Another factor which influences the reporting of rape to police is the amount of property the rapist steals. The more the property has stolen, the more likely the victim is to report a rape to police (Bourque, 1989:48.)

Russell (1974:36) also suggests that in USA more rapes occur with women in minority groups who are alienated from the police.

The victims do not wish to go to court because of judicial processes – like a woman having to prove that the attack was against her will and that she did resist the attack. Prosecutors also intimidate raped women by probing the victim's sexual past, which is humiliating and embarrassing. It is also reported that educated women often do not report rape to police in fear of spoiling their reputation.

The procedure, as Part et al (1993:28) suggest, seems very harrowing and many women avoid reporting rape, considering the trauma that it involves. In many rape trials the issue becomes whether or not the victim consented to sexual intercourse. The determination of consent can lead to distressing cross-examinations of the rape victims in court. Due to lack of sufficient evidence, those charged with the crime have a higher rate of acquittal.

As Temkin (1995) suggests, the victim's evidence in most cases is not believed, and this discourages women from reporting cases of rape. Temkin claims that the legal system excludes the experience of women; for instance a woman's failure to complain of rape within a reasonable time after the *fact,* raises a strong objection to the rape charge (p 279). She also claims that attempted rapes are more frequently reported than completed rapes; and that in USA non-whites are likely to report rapes to police than whites; though black women do not report when the rapist is a white man.

In Britain, young white girls are 30 times more likely to be raped than women over 45. Francome claims that this is similar to USA figures, where women aged 16-19 are more than three times likely to be raped than those aged 35.

In USA black women are twice more likely to be raped than white women. Lea et al (1984:31) argue that a poor black woman whose income is $3,000 is almost six times more likely to be raped than a rich white woman whose income is $25,000. It is argued that being in a lower class and being black and young puts a woman at a great risk of being raped in USA.

Scully (1990:65) suggests that the number of rapists is higher in the working-class. She further points out that the number might be higher because the men within the lower class do not have money to pay the sophisticated lawyers who can beat the charges.

It is claimed that racism is felt in police and the judicial systems in as far as rape is concerned. Russell (1975:291) points out that if a victim is white, and the rapist is black, the usual rigorous requirements of proof that exist when the rapist is white are lifted so that the rapist is more likely to be found guilty.

However, if the victim is black and the rapist is white, the victim is likely to be subjected to a far harsher and more unfair trial than her white sister. Russell further points out that in cases where racism and sexism are combined, it is unlikely that a white man would be convicted for raping a black woman. (Russell 1984:290-1).

There is a prevalent view of male authors, clinicians and doctors, policemen and prosecutors, that women enjoy being raped, and even when raped they do not report their rapes. The authors base their view on the feelings of rape victims – like experiencing orgasm. Segal (1990:235) claims that the prevalence of rape as a social practice exists precisely because of the myths surrounding it.

Many men believe that a woman cannot be raped; and that rape only happens to victims who ask for it (Amir, 1971:161). It is further believed that a woman can resist rape because of the position of her sexual organs, except where she is intoxicated or surprised by the attacker. Furthermore, it is argued that women's physical and verbal resistance is seen as part of the female game of pretending reluctance, or as an expression of the desire to be overcome (Amir1971:162). It is claimed that when women say "No", men think its a societal "No" and think the woman wants to be coaxed. Men further allege that all women say "no" when they mean "yes", so that they do not feel responsible later (Scully, 1990:120).

This argument, however, is rubbished by Russell (1984:257-8), claiming that men are stronger and faster than women. Russell points out that some rapists appear to want to turn the woman on physically, as well as win her emotionally. On the issue of orgasm, Russell claims that women fake orgasm due to the frightening position they are in. Russell quotes one of the women she interviewed, who told her:

*"He wanted me to have an orgasm. When I finally figured out that he wouldn't come until I did, I just pretended that I had an orgasm." (*Russell, 1984:110)

Russell also points out that rape is related to the different way women and men are raised. She argues that men have been trained to be physical and assertive whereas women have been trained to be passive, weak, respectful to men and non-violent. Russell further claims that if women were physically stronger than men, there would not be many instances of men raping women.

Susan Edwards (1981:24-5) adds that femininity is desired from the model of passivity. This, she argues, produced a discourse that provided for a passive construction of gender and social roles. A good woman is devoted to her family, to domestic work and to the adoration of her husband. She is to acknowledge and recognise her husband's supreme position, and she is expected to be obedient and subservient (p25).

However, Amir (1971:155) does not exonerate women entirely. He argues that a woman failing to take preventive measures – like the failure to react strongly enough against sexual suggestions, or agreeing voluntarily to drink or ride with a stranger – makes her accountable for falling victim to rape.

The second myth is that rape is a crime caused by uncontrollable sex drive. Karpman(1951:190) refers to the rapists as sexual psychopaths and argues that they don't act consciously. He argues that rapists don't deliberately carry out acts of rape, but rather that they are victims of illness. It is further argued that men who are in prison for several rapes are unable to control their sex drive.

Scully (1994) claims that this myth became so popular (as an accepted explanation as to why men rape) that it encouraged them to rape women more, since they (men) were not held responsible for it.

This argument, however, is refuted by (Holmes, 1991:74). He argues that such men who are referred to as 'sick' are married and have their sex partners when they commit such crimes. So it is wrong to say that they rape because they are unable to control their sex drive. Brownmiller, too, refutes this argument and points out that Gang rapes should prove this myth a lie. (Brownmiller, 1975:313)

Another myth which is widely believed is that *rapes are committed by strangers* Russell (1974:257). Walker (1988:27) refutes this claim, and argues that 50 per cent of all sexual assaults on adult women are committed by men who know their victims. He further claims that as high as 80 per cent of rape cases are in situations where the rapists are known to their victims. For instance, date-rape, acquaintance-rape and marital-rape are examples of rape cases where the rapist is known to the victim.

As Amir (1971:142) suggests, most rapes are planned. He claims that in his sample of 646 rapes, 72 per cent were planned, 12 per cent were partially planned, and 16 per cent were an exclusive event.

Bart et al (1993:114) claims that in USA there are far more rapes than come to public attention. Rapes occur in fraternity houses and in colleges and university campuses.

Rape is a common event which is often planned by the rapist, who usually has a wife or regular girlfriend and therefore is not sex-starved. He does not attack a stranger but a woman he knows (Segal, 1990:235).

The fourth myth is that *women report false rapes* – malicious rape accusations – and when taken to court, more often than not, the alleged rapist is found innocent and acquitted. It is believed that women have a propensity for falsifying charges of sexual offences by men – hoping that juries would be more sympathetic to the victim (Galvin, 1986:788).

To the contrary, Holmes (1991:74) argues that it is more likely for women not to report a rape that has occurred, as they themselves may face a lot of embarrassment and humiliation when they make such charges.

Segal (1990) claims that the police, hospitals, and judicial treatment of rape victims is frequently hostile to the assaulted woman, and more protective of the 'rights' of the rapist than the rights of the woman. Segal argues that the woman should be allowed – at any time in any place – to say 'NO' to sex.

Segal further charges that men are 'shock troops' of patriarchy, necessary for male domination (Segal, 1990:236). In this, Segal further supports Brownmiller's claim that: *"rape is nothing more or less than a conscious process of intimidation by which all men keep* all women *in a state of fear"* (Brownmiller,1975:15) (emphasis is mine).

However, Brownmiller's claim that all men are

potential rapists has been rejected by her fellow feminists as extreme. Segal (1990) argues that rape in different societies varies considerably, and she contrasts societies which are relatively rape-free, like Sumatra, with those which are most rape-prone, like the United States.

In rape-free societies, Segal argues, women are respected and are influential members of the community, participating in public decision-making, and the relationship between the sexes tends to be symmetrical and equal.

Toner (1982) argues that rape is due to the patterns of relationship within the society, and between the sexes. She points out that there is separateness and hostility between men and women right from childhood. Boys are socialised differently from the girls, and sex roles start from childhood.

This leads me to suggest some social changes that can reduce rates of rape. As Matthews (1994) suggests, reducing rape would need changing gender relations because rape, battering, incest and other forms of violence are rooted in the power men have over women. As Segal (1990) suggests, both gender structures and consciousness must be changed. She claims that the problem of rape has to do with the question of the position of women in society.

As Russell(1994:274) suggests, if males and females were to be liberated from their sexual roles, the rape situation would change drastically. Sex equality in the society should be promoted, so that woman and man can look at each other as equals. Both the male and female would value sex within the relationship more than sex for its own sake. Sex equality should include the levels of physical, educational, economic, political, and psychological well-being of the woman in society.

This can be achieved through "rape-prevention" education programmes. Seminars and conferences related to rape and sexual assaults should be organised so that the community is sensitised on rape issues.

As Medea et al (1974) suggest, anti-rape Women organisations and Movements which are vital in dealing with the problems of rape should be set up and supported by the State. These groups should take initiative to force changes in men and in the structures they control. Society should be educated that rape is not an isolated act of an aberrant individual, but a crime against women that is encouraged by a sexist society (Brownmiller, 1975:125). *"Treat the society then you have treated the rapist",* claims Russell (1974:292).

Education should be extended to the police force, the law courts, hospitals and other established institutions so that they can change their attitudes towards rape victims. Medea and his colleagues also suggest that Rape-Squads should be established in Police Stations. Important, too, are Rape-crisis call lines which should be established in most areas, so that women can easily call police immediately in case of rape. Effective action should be taken against racism in the police force and the courts.

Meadea (1974) further suggests that the Rape crisis centres would focus public attention on the problem of rape. These centres would support the usually isolated rape victims, provide rape counselling services and, above all, provide information about rape.

As Bart et al (1993:260) suggest, there must be spousal equality in marriage so that women are not solely responsible for domestic work, child care and emotional and psychological support. If the wife in the family is given equal responsibility to make important decisions, it would reduce the man's pride of being the supreme authority in the family. This should involve the changing of the society's attitudes towards sex roles. Spousal equality in marriage would also reduce women's continued economic dependence on their husbands. It is important to eliminate the gender gap income, which results from the low wage rates paid in female-centred occupations, compared to the male-dominated occupations where men earn higher wages for the same level of training and skills as women. (Bart, 1993:260-3).

Rape must be redefined as violence so that it can be treated more seriously by state organs. The state should put in place laws which do not blame the victim. The court requirements which humiliate and embarrass the victims should be removed. This will encourage more reporting of rape and consequent sentencing of rapists (Matthews, 1994:150), which in turn will reduce the rate of rape.

As Baron et al (1989) point out, the demoralising and brutalising poverty and economic inequality should be eradicated, for it is suggested that violent crime is associated with poverty, and rapists are more likely to come from areas with the greatest poverty and urban decay. Therefore, reducing poverty levels – which is usually accompanied by economic inequality – would reduce rates of rape (Baron, 1989:194).

Social disorganisation reduces social constraints against rape (Baron 1989). Therefore, to reduce rape, the community and family ties should be strengthened to create new neighbourhood-based organs which provide social support and social control of the traditional institutions.

Since male judges handle rape cases unfairly, female judges and female attorneys should be appointed, and juries with sexist attitudes should not be appointed. Government should compensate rape victims, as this would be an incentive for rape victims to report rape cases. As a result, more rapists would be caught and it would reduce the rates of rape.

Women doctors should be available for the medical examination of rape victims if the woman or the court requests for it (Hall, 1985).

Hall (1985:154) also suggests that housing policies should aim at providing re-housing for women who run away to escape rape by their husbands. Suitable accommodation should be provided without much delay.

Chapter Nine

DOMESTIC VIOLENCE:
Living in the House of Horrors

Miranda Davies defines domestic violence as a variety of actions and omissions that occur in different relationships. The term is narrowly used to cover incidents of physical attack and sexual violence.

These attacks do not just happen violently; they begin as small cases of abuse and grow, thus leading to physical, psychological or mental violence. These may consist of verbal abuse, harassment, confinement, rape, beatings, and deprivation of contacts with friends and family members, among others.

According to the publication by the Department of Women in Development, at the Ministry of Women in Development, Culture and Youth, domestic violence involves the use of force on members of the family, like hitting, beating, cutting or other ways of causing pain to the person. It also involves other ways intended to cause suffering to a person, for example denying a person basic necessities of life such as food, medical care, using abusive language intended to humiliate that person.

Domestic violence is a phenomenon that is universal and affects all people, that is men, women and children. However, women are the most likely victims to the extent that at the mention of domestic violence, one thinks of women being ill-treated.

Domestic Violence against Women

Violence against women is manifested in political, social, economic and private spheres of life.

Politically, during political upheavals, women are often raped and brutalized.

Socially, cultural norms and practices affect women's rights. Because men pay bride price, they think they own a woman, and that she has to dance to their tune. However, though married, a woman remains an individual like any other with individual human rights that are inviolable and which are protected by the state against abuse by anyone.

Female circumcision in other customs is also a practice that shows social violence on women. This is usually enforced by traditional/clan leaders or family members but it is a violation of the woman/girl's rights in the light of the modern developments that highlight the medical dangers that lie in female circumcision which affect her negatively, especially if carried out against her will, as these would impact on her in later life, affecting her functions in marriage. Some NGOs have had to come from outside to intervene on behalf of women where the state has been powerless to legislate against traditional practices for political reasons even when the human rights concerns are obvious.

Most of the perpetuators of violence against women are members of the household or the community where the victim lives. However, women also face violence in their work places. For example, before they are given a job, bosses may first ask a female job seeker to sleep with them, or when employed, the bosses ask them to sleep with them before their salaries are increased or before they are promoted, or as a security for their jobs. Some of this sexual abuse may appear trivial and light-hearted and jocular – like passing remarks or whistles – but they often reach a level when they should not be tolerated, particularly when they are indulged in by junior staff who must be disciplined before it gets out of hand. Whatever the case, a woman has a right to work without harassment of any kind and it is the duty of her employers to ensure that every woman in their employment is guaranteed a peaceful, productive work environment free of innuendo or any other abusive interferences. Legal action to enforce this should be a last resort when internal interventions have failed.

Domestic Violence against Children

Children also suffer domestic violence. Abandonment by the adults responsible for their protection is one form of domestic violence children face. This is common in towns and cities where economic and social problems are severe. In such situations, children are usually abandoned by unmarried mothers or mothers who are married but are themselves abandoned by husbands. It also happens when the mothers are prostitutes, schoolgirls, mentally-disturbed, parents with problems themselves and stepmothers who refuse or reject responsibility for the children concerned. Children's homes and other institutions have become a haven of abandoned babies of a more tender-age. In Mulago Hospital, every two months there is a baby abandoned in the wards or on the premises. In Naguru Remand Home, out of the many children under care and protection, at least twenty have been abandoned by their parents or relatives, for example an eight year old boy who had originally lived in Banda was picked up by police at the Kampala Bus Park where he had been abandoned by his stepmother. The under-aged who are old enough to walk the streets are simply left on their own to survive through begging for food and finding their own shelter and clothing with all the innumerable risks it entails.

Child labour is also a form of domestic violence against children. In African societies in general, children begin working as soon as they learn to walk. They labour in the farms, herd cattle, and do craft work. When they are as old as nine years, they are taken by city dwellers at the consent of their parents to go and work for their richer relatives in the city or suburbs. Girls face this fate more often than boys who are more likely to continue with their education. These girls often end up being sexually and physically abused to the extent that others run away only to wind up becoming prostitutes or embracing a life of crime that brings their childhood to a close.

Domestic Violence against Men

Men have usually been thought of solely as the perpetrators of domestic violence on women. However, men also suffer domestic violence. In 2003, the Uganda Human Rights Commission tracked newspaper reports on domestic violence which revealed a worrying extent of the incidence of violence by women against their spouses. The findings revealed in *The Monitor* and *New Vision* newspapers indicated that 120 cases of domestic violence showed that 40% of those against men were perpetrated by women. For example, in 2003 it was reported that a woman cut off her husband's penis because she suspected him of having had an extra-marital affair. It is true that women sometimes retaliate against their abusers by killing them. However, Straus found that only 10% of women and 15% of men perpetuate partner-abuse in self-defence.

Other men suffer regular abuse by being denied sexual intercourse or threatened with death while others lose their jobs when their wives connive with their employers to penalise them for reasons that can range from greed to sexual abuse.

Social Background to Domestic Violence

In a survey conducted at Queens' University, by Pamela Montgomery showed that most women regarded wife-battering as a normal part of married life. Out of the 181 female staff she questioned, a quarter opposed any sentence against a man who beats his wife if the couple has been married for over twenty years.

Studies carried out in ten countries, between 38% and 70% of women have suffered physical assaults by a partner. Other forms are domestic abuse are rape, child marriages, and female circumcision. Expressed preference of the male child to the female is also a case of domestic violence which affects women in the whole world but is most serious in Asia where it is often life-threatening. Its consequences are said to be anything from fatal of female infanticide to neglect of the girl child over the boy child in terms of essential needs such as nutrition, basic health care and education.

In India every year on average five women are killed in dowry-related disputes and many more cases are never reported.

The discovery of domestic violence against women is a problem rooted in the structure of the social order, rather than the pathological psyches of individual men and as an important component of feminist theories that has taken different paths in different parts of the world. This discovery coincided with the early stages in the development of feminist theories on gender relations.

In other parts of the world, it was the United Nations decade for women 1975-1985 that became the primary catalyst for discovering domestic violence against women. Gray Ford's study shows that women have been punished, kicked, attacked with knives, and broken bottles, beaten with belts and buckles, burned and sealed. All the research that has been done on the extent of domestic violence worldwide clearly shows that this is a global problem affecting women in all forms of cultures. In the U.S.A. alone, it is estimated that one third to one half of all women who live with male companions experience forms of brutality such as threats of severe harm, degradation, beatings and torture. The results show that a high incidence of domestic violence was linked to alcohol-abuse. Most of the women had been married for ten years or more before they reported to either the hospital or the police; and twenty percent of the assaults were related to accusations of extra-marital affairs on the part of one of the spouses. A third of the women were illiterate, two thirds had some schooling but none had University education.

In the world, the idea that a man is superior to the woman has not been eliminated. Underestimation and discrimination of women still exist.

In Brazil, the authorities pushed for Domestic violence in cases of extra-marital sex. The defence of honour in Brazil, prior to Brazil's independence in 1822, Portuguese colonial rule allowed a man who caught his wife in an act of adultery to kill her and her lover, although the reverse was not true. Therefore, the problem of domestic violence is a worldwide phenomenon.

Max Weber defines "sexual relationship" as "Harrschaft", meaning a relationship of dominance and subordinate status. A critical examination of sexual relationships today and in history shows that it all falls in this category as defined by Weber.

Myth has it that once upon a time there was equality

and perfect harmony between men and women in African societies. There was also equitable division of labour: the men went out to hunt or look after livestock while the women stayed at home and provided food and care for the family. It was from this division of labour itself that tensions later grew as men's roles started to dominate while the women remained subordinate. By the time the monetary economy was introduced with the coming of Europeans, men were in a better position to grab the opportunities that saw them continue to lead and literally hold the women under subjection.

In the case of Uganda, Jjuko asserts that a husband more or less had the power of life and death over his wife. Ignorance and myths were the major causes of domestic violence in pre-colonial Uganda. For example, a menstruating woman was considered almost unholy, too unclean to cook food or to come in the presence of her husband or to touch anything that was a symbol of power, yet failing to menstruate called for the wounding the unfortunate wife and such a woman was considered the cause of the barrenness of the soil.

Men were polygamous and that was a sign of their wealth. However, a woman was meant to be faithful to one husband. This was common among the Batooro and the Banyoro where on the acquisition of more wealth, the man would acquire another wife. The first was treated as a wife, while others as more or less servants. Among the Banyankole, monogamy was the rule and polygamy the exception for men. However, polygamy appears to have come up as a result of barrenness. If a woman failed to produce, then her sister would be brought in to produce children for her husband.

During the colonial era in Uganda, the clan ties were weakened and the lineage became social units with a man as its head. This was because change in the economy from the socialistic to the capitalist. Each family had to produce commodities with surplus for sale to pay taxes and pay for other basic needs, including education for his children. It was the men who could work on plantations to earn money to support the family. Women stayed at home to provide food for the family. This lowered the status of women. Because power depended on the money economy, women became dependants since they did not work for money. Thus men could do anything they wanted with their dependants, which prompted domestic violence.

Even after independence nothing was done to reduce this dependence since the institutions were weak. Thus tolerance of the domestic violence was the only solution. Tradition could not allow men to divorce, and the institutions to which to report violence were inaccessible by women who had no money, and they were too weak to raise any objections. They thus had to cope with domestic violence.

Causes of Domestic Violence

One of the causes of domestic violence in urban societies is the informal marriages that many young people go into. These cohabitations are not legally recognized as marriage. Some girls just jump into these relationships without considering the consequences. It is no wonder some men then take advantage and treat these girls like servants. They face more domestic violence compared to women in legally recognized marriages. Because they are afraid that the man might marry another wife, such women usually choose to cope with brutality. But if a girl has introduced her partner to her parents and relatives, her husband would value her and treat her with respect for fear of her parents and relatives. Even when he treats her badly, she knows that she can go back to her parents if the situation became intolerable.

Alcohol abuse has been highlighted as the cause of most domestic violence in marital relationships. It is often said that when men get drunk, they become irritable and their tempers flare up with the smallest provocation. In that condition they want everything done as they command. For example, in one case documented by the Legal Aid project of the Uganda Law Society, a woman who had brought a complaint against her husband for assaulting her whenever he was drunk explained that he also assaulted the children by locking them out of the house and threatening to kill them. In *The Monitor* newspaper of 27th November 1986, a drunken man returned home and under that influence almost beat up his wife to death. The wife as a result could not cook food for the children or efficiently execute her other duties or household chores.

Lack of good communication in the home is also another cause of domestic violence. Men think that women should not talk to them or explain anything to them. Any mistake is solved by beating up the woman without listening to her explanation. Thus the stronger men exploit their strength to batter their weaker wives.

This gender power imbalance has sustained domestic violence in Uganda. There is a belief that the husband is always right and never makes mistakes. Men use even their legal position to sustain domestic violence on women. At the FIDA Legal Aid Clinic of the Uganda Association of Women Lawyers, there was a case of a retired police officer who had sent away his wife for over years ago but continued to molest her, which eventually led to his being charged with battery, prosecuted and imprisoned.

Children grow up seeing their parents fighting. They think it is normal and that a woman who is not beaten is not loved. Boys take it up when they marry while girls are made to accept that it is wrong to complain of being beaten since it is a sign of love. Some of these young people find themselves living with domestic violence without knowing that it is a criminal offence for which there is recourse in the law courts.

Women are expected to be submissive to sexual demands even when these are made under unreasonable circumstances. They are expected to tolerate sexual abuse and when they report to their elders, they are asked to do as demanded because it is their role in the marriage. Often cases of domestic violence do not reach formal dispute resolution because of under-reporting, laxity and condoning which to a large extent fuels domestic violence.

The economic dependence of women on men is another cause of domestic violence – both physical and psychological. Men take advantage of women's lack of economic resources to inflict violence on them. In a High Court criminal session Case No 79 of 1993, Uganda Vs Night Kinkuhaire, the accused was convicted of manslaughter after she admitted killing her child by drowning in the swamp. The Judge sentenced her to 12 months imprisonment. Counsel for the accused submitted that the accused had committed the offence because an unwanted child was a burdened she could not bear alone. The extreme act of taking her child's life was out of extreme hardship inflicted on her by the father of the child who refused to pay any maintenance.

Insecurity is another cause of domestic violence. Nevwirth observes that in armed conflicts, rape has been used as a weapon of war whenever there is civic upheaval. This happens all over the world. These women feel helpless and suffer trauma as a result of rape by the rebels or army. In one such case, a woman Hanuna says: "The army raped me when my son, 27 years old, man was watching. I felt like taking my life. My son suffered trauma more than I did. He is still mourning the taking away of my dignity and integrity." Such women, who have nothing to do with the cause of war, end up suffering most.

Forced marriages also cause domestic violence. Some men, against their will, are forced to marry girls they impregnated. Such men see these girls not as wives but as a burden and treat them with brutality. The man ends up taking another wife just to hurt the girl he has been made to marry. Other women are threatened with death. Salama (2000) states: "I do not have love for my husband. I have been forced to marry a man who I have not been in a relationship with. I would like to marry my former boyfriend whom I love so much but my husband swore to kill me if I leave him. He knows I am not comfortable in my marriage."

Some enlightened women suffer domestic violence because their husbands force them to become pregnant and bear more children than they can look after. If they try to use contraceptives, they are beaten until they give in to their husband's demands.

Bride wealth is another cause of domestic violence. The payment of dowry, which is meant to be an appreciation to the parents of the girl, has turned into a transaction in which the man is forced to pay a lot of money in lieu of cows. After acquiring the girl, he treats her like an item he has bought. She is property he owns. In this regard the practice of bride price as an expression of unbalanced gender power relations endorses domestic violence.

Unfaithfulness in a marriage is another common cause of domestic violence. Men often suspect their wives of unfaithfulness, especially if the woman is working. Such men don't want the women to leave the home on their own to go anywhere. When they women disobey, they are beaten violently. Also, when women find out that the man are unfaithful and complain about it, they are beaten by their husbands for daring to follow their movements.

Men feel they own the women and that they should therefore decide on each detail of the women's lives, thus allowing them no rights whatsoever. For example, during elections, women face a lot of domestic violence if they support an opponent of the candidate their husbands support. In a case reported by *The New Vision* newspaper on 24 May 1996, a man from Arua district offered his wife in an election bet over which candidate would win. When he lost, he was asked to hand over the woman to honour the bet. In another case in Mukono, a man killed his wife for supporting a different candidate from the one he wanted her to vote for. Such men don't recognise even the basic rights of the woman as an individual and as a citizen of this country.

Effects of Domestic Violence

Ms Robinson, a former United Nations High Commissioner for Human Rights, notes that violence against the woman throughout her life cycle derives essentially from cultural patterns, in particular the harmful effects of certain traditions and customary practices as well as acts of extremism linked to race, sex, language or religion that perpetuate the lower status accorded to women in the family, the workplace, the community and in society at large.

Domestic violence against women has clear effects. Apart from suffering minor physical injuries like bruising or more serious ones like the breaking of limbs that go unreported, in the extreme women often suffer death. The serious effects of domestic violence include health and psychological injury that can last a lifetime if not treated. Such women suffer a significantly higher level of anxiety, depression and somatic complaints than women who have never suffered abuse. Many of them get paralyzed because of the threats of attack and the daily stress they live under. They are most likely to be deprived, which leads to higher rates of suicide than those found among women who have not been battered.

Domestic violence results in severe and most times permanent health problems for the women affected. One woman, who was forced to have sexual intercourse during her menstrual periods, suffered an increase of severe bleeding that extended from three days to weeks, with severe pain in her lower abdomen.

Other women complain of having endured childbirths when they were still very young due to forced sexual intercourse, others suffer from trauma because of tension and worry over whether they are pregnant or not. Some of these women are susceptible to domestic violence when they get married to men who cannot understand that they have a problem that needs to be attended to.

Some women commit criminal offences on their husbands as the only way of getting relief from domestic violence. These women at times do in self-defence and end up in prison. The killing of abusive husbands by their wives is not confined to developed countries exists worldwide. There are many women prisoners who are incarcerated because they have murdered husbands who have abused them.

Children who grow up in such a kind of family have a likelihood of being affected physically, mentally or psychologically. When they try to protect or defend their mother, some of them are injured or get killed in the process while those who survive grow up hating their fathers.

A Canadian study suggests that witnessing parental conflict and violence during childhood is significantly predictive of serious adult personal crimes like murder, kidnapping, assault, rape and robbery in later life. Other children like that get chased out of their homes and become street children while others, on beginning families of their own later in life, find themselves practicing the same acts of violence.

Loss of property by women is also a possible result of

domestic violence. Women's property is often confiscated without compensation by their husbands and these women thus end up not saving anything. These losses can vary from small savings like livestock to big items like houses which they jointly owned with their husbands who connived not to have that ownership legally recognised. Some women lose actual cash from their salaries or from sale of produce from their investments which the men they are married to or cohabit with either spend on alcohol or on other women.

Domestic violence often leads to many women finally deciding to dissolve marriage and save their lives, leaving their children behind. Men in such situations marry other women, who treat the children badly by starving them, beating them, which also thus leads to other forms of domestic violence. Such children thus grow up with much hatred for their father and stepmother, who sometimes end up killing them.

Families living in conditions of domestic violence are often economically poor since the wife is always running away from the husband and the little she saves is taken away from her forcefully. As a result, the children drop out of school and the family becomes dependent on other people, especially relatives.

The government also bears the brunt of domestic violence. Expenditure increases on strengthening institutions which are created to protect the rights of women and curbing domestic violence. One Canadian estimate suggests that in 1980, Canadian taxpayers through their local government paid at least 32 million Canadian Dollars for police intervention on cases of wife beating and for related support and administrative services. Similarly, an Australian study found that the cost of service for twenty victims of domestic violence was well over one million Australian Dollars.

Stepmothers mistreat children who are left behind by their mothers. For example, twelve year old Brenda was allegedly told to make a fire in the kitchen by her stepmother after which the stepmother, with the help of her real daughter, Brenda's stepsister, tied her up and hang her above the fire, locked her up in the room and went away.

Domestic violence has caused an increase in street children in cities and towns. According to the research done on street children in Kampala, by 1989 their estimated numbers were put at between three hundred and eight hundred (UNICEF Report). In 1992 NGOs and government estimated the total number of street children in Kampala to be one thousand out of two thousand in the whole country. In 1993 there was a worsening situation with the number going up to 1147 street children in the city and its suburbs.

Mothers drop their children on the streets when they fail to maintain them after their husbands have ignored them. A young mother, aged twenty-five, of Kabowa appeared before a Kampala Magistrate for abandoning her four-year-old son at the Kampala Railway Station. Her defence was that her husband was not assisting her in maintaining the child.

Recommendations/Remedies

Society should be educated about domestic violence so that people can report all cases to the police or other organizations for intervention. Community members should also support the victims of domestic violence to survive instead of merely gossiping about them.

Psychologists and workers in organizations dealing with these victims should be trained to offer them comfort and health facilities instead of being unsympathetic towards them. Through seminars and other forms of training, these agencies should be made to understand that the issues involved are not only domestic but an infringement of God-given rights that involve torture, cruelty, inhumanity and degrading punishment. It is the duty of these agencies to protect the human rights of these victims.

Laws should be reformed with clearly stipulated punishment for people who practice domestic violence. The laws in place should be enforced and judicial officers should handle these cases seriously by giving heavy punishments which will lead to the reduction in domestic violence cases in society. Biased response and discriminatory behaviour on the part of the officials and court personnel must be quickly identified and dealt with. Family courts or any other specialist courts should be set up to guarantee the speedy trials as well as an effort to ensure privacy through simple and sympathetic procedures.

Once this is established, victims would be encouraged to report cases of domestic violence without fear or ridicule. They would know that their rights are protected and that they are assured of being given humane treatment. It is only when they are treated like human beings that they will come out and report their victimisers and it is only then that the organizations that are out to help them will know who need help and intervene on their behalf.

Violence against women must be seen as a problem of society as a whole and not just the women affected.. Therefore, all programs that aim at stopping domestic violence should involve men as well and sensitize them about its effects on their families and on society. Unless men change their negative attitudes, domestic violence will continue to exist.

Medical officers who deal with patients who are victims of domestic violence should be trained on how to help those victims medically and by encouraging them not to fear to report their cases to the police or concerned organization. The medical records should show statistics with a gender breakdown.

REFERENCES

Allers, et al (1992): Unresolved childhood sexual abuse: Are older adults affected? Journal of Counseling and development.71 (1), 14-17.

Andrew J. et al (1998): "Effects of Parental Divorce on Mental Health Throughout the Life Course," *American Sociological Review*, Vol. 63 (April 1998), pp. 245–246.

Armsworth, et al (1993): The effects of psychological trauma on children and adolescents; Journal of counseling and development, 72(1) 49-54.

ARW (2001): Human Rights Watch; Humanity Denied; Systematic Violation of Women's Rights in Afghanistan; New York.

ARW (1996): Human Rights Watch, over coming Fear; Human Rights Violation Against Women In Mexico; Newyork.

Barton, U et al (1994): Equity and vulnerability; A situation Analysis of women, adolescents and Children in Uganda. Kampala:

Bohannon C, (1968): Marriage, Family and Residence, Garden City New York.

Brown, S.A et al (1995). Stress, vulnerability, and adult alcohol relapse. Journal of Studies on Alcohol 56(5):538-545, 1995.

Brown, S.A, et al (1990): Severity of psychosocial stress and outcome of alcoholism treatment. *Journal of*

Abnormal Psychology 99(4):344-348.

Brown, S.A, et al (1990) Severity of psychosocial stress and outcome of alcoholism treatment. *Journal of Abnormal Psychology* 99(4):344-348.

David P. F (1990): "Implications of Criminal Career Research for the Prevention of Offending," *Journal of Adolescence*, Vol. 13 , pp. 93–113.

Draft social welfare policy of the department of probation and social welfare (1994). A publication of the ministry of social welfare.

Edith C et al (1991), "The Long Term Effects of Divorce on Children: A Review," *Journal of the American Academy of Child Adolescent Psychiatry*, Vol. 30 (1991), pp. 349–360.

Eskay, R.L. (2001). The effects of alcohol on selected regulatory aspects of the stress axis. Leeds, England. A& M publishers.

Frank *Namangale, (2005), The article "Legalise homosexuality says Human rights body" The Daily News (Malawi).*

Freud, S. (1961). *The Complete Works of Sigmund Freud* (Vol. 19). London : Hogarth.

Friendreich E (1884): The Origin of the Family, Private Property, and the State, page.118.

Grych, J. H. et al (1992). Interventions for children of divorce: Toward greater integration of research and action. *Psychological Bulletin, 111*, 424-454.

Higley, J.D. (2001). Primate model of alcohol abuse: Effects of early experience, personality, and stress on alcohol consumption. Proceedings of the National Academy of Sciences U.S.A. 88:7261-7265, 2001.

Hogg,R, S et al (1997) *International Journal of Epidemiology* (vol. 27, no. 3, pp 657-661)

Higley, J.D. (2001). Primate model of alcohol abuse: Effects of early experience, personality, and stress on alcohol consumption. Proceedings of the National Academy of Sciences U.S.A. 88:7261-7265.

Hilakivi-C, L. et al (2002).: Social status and voluntary alcohol consumption in mice: Interaction with stress. New York, USA; Psychopharmacology Publications.

Hilakivi-Clarke, et al (2002): Social status and voluntary alcohol consumption in mice: Interaction with stress. New York, USA; Psychopharmacology Publications.

Human Rights Watch (1999):, Crime or Customs; Violence Against Women In Tanzania, New York.

Human Rights Watch (2000): Seeking Protection; Addressing Social and Domestic Violence In Tanzanian Refugee Camps, New York.

Hunt, W. et al (1995) Stress, Gender, *and Alcohol-Seeking Behaviour,* National Institute on Alcohol Abuse and Alcoholism Research Monograph No 29. Bethesda.

Daling J.R et.al,(1982), "Correlates of Homosexual Behavior and the Incidence of Anal Cancer," *Journal of the American Medical Association* 247, no.14.

Jaffe et al (1986): Emotional and Psychical Health Problems of Battered Women; Canadian Jovial of Psychiatry No.31 .

Jennison, K.M. (2002). The impact of stressful life events and social support on drinking among older adults: A general population survey. International Journal of Aging and Human Development 35(2):99-123, 2002.

Jennison, K.M. (2002): The impact of stressful life events and social support on drinking among older adults: A general population survey. International Journal of Aging and Human Development 35(2):99-123.

Julie C Harren (2004) Educating the public on the causes of homosexuality, NARTH collected papers.

Kabanza, M et al (1994): A final report of a study on the contribution of children to family income in Uganda; ministry of finance and economic planning for alleviation of poverty and social costs of adjustment.

Kaggwa J F (1998) : Domestic Violence Against Women in Uganda.

Kaggwa J. F (1998): Domestic Violence Against Women in Uganda.

Kalant, H. (2000). Stress-related effects of ethanol in mammals. Critical Reviews in Biotechnology 9(4):265-272, 2000.

Kalant, H. (2000). Stress-related effects of ethanol in mammals. Critical Reviews in Biotechnology 9(4):265, 272

Kaleman,(1965): Report of commission on marriage, divorce and the status of women.

Kasl, S.V. et al (2001), The impact of the accident at the Three Mile Island on the behavior and well-being of nuclear workers. Part II: Job tension, psychophysiological symptoms, and indices of distress. American Journal of Public Health 71(5):484-495, 2001.

Legal Aid project report of Uganda law society 1993 \to 1995.

Margaret S (1993: Country report for the seminar on improvement of the status of women.

Mbazira J,, (2003): Woman cuts off hubby's penis;

Monitor newspaper 20th December , Uganda.

Mbazira, J, (2003): Woman cuts off hubby's penis;

Monitor newspaper 20th December 2003.

Moove, S. et al (1995): Sexuality in adolescents: adolescence and society series. London, New York: Routledge.

Nash, J.F. (1998). <u>The role of the hypothalamic-pituitary-adrenocortical axis in post-stress induced ethanol consumption by youths</u>. Leeds University, England: Leeds University press.

Nevwirth, G. (1997): Women Refugees In International Perspective, Research Resource Division For Refugees, Ottawa.

New Vision 1st August 1989.

New Vision, November 14th 1995.

Pamela J. S, (1993): "The Economic Costs of Marital Disruption for Young Women over the Past Two Decades." Demography 30,pp 353-371.

Paul Cameron-PhD (1997) What Causes Homosexual desire and can it be Changed? The Family Research Report newsletter. Colorado, Springs.

Phillip W.C. (1998). *The Hidden Side of Domestic Violence,* Place, Publishers,

Phillip W.Cook ;(1998) (The hidden Side of Domestic Violence; 1998 .

Plotsky, P.M et al (2003). Increased plasma ACTH responses to stress in nonhandled compared with handled rats require basal levels of corticosterone and are associated with increased levels of ACTH secretagogues in the median eminence. Manchester, England: The Journal of Neuroscience.

Pohorecky, L.A. (2001): Stress and alcohol interaction: An update of human research. Alcoholism: Clinical and Experimental Research 15(3):438-459

Pope John Paul II (1979): "Theology of the body" – a collection of 129 addresses delivered between September 1979 and November 1984 .

Rivier, C. (2000): Prolonged exposure to alcohol: Effect on CRF and RNA levels, and CRF- and stress-induced ACTH secretion in the rat, Brain Research 520: 1-5. maimi

Robinson B,A, (1997) : Homosexuality and other Sexual Orientations: Speculations into causes.

Sadava, S.W. et al (1993). <u>Stress-related problem drinking and alcohol problems</u>. Edmonton, Canada: Macmillan Publishers.

Satinover, J. (1996). The gay gene? *The Journal of Human Sexuality.*

Spencer, R.L et al (2004): <u>Adaptation of the hypothalamic-pituitary-adrenal axis to chronic ethanol stress</u>, Macmillan publishers, London.

Syed M, (2007) The effects of pornography and homosexuality on society. Muslim Unity.

The monitor 20th January 1997: Rape in South Africa blames on brutalizes society.

The Monitor 23rd march 1997.

The Monitor 7th January 1997.

The New vision 16th June 1996.

The New vision newspaper 29th October 1996.

Uganda Human Rights Commission (2003): 6th Annual Report.

UN (1995): Women And Violence; Geneva, United Nations Department Of Public Information.

Volpicelli, J.R. (1997) :Uncontrollable events and alcohol drinking. London, England: Longman publishers.

Volpicelli, J.R. (1997). Uncontrollable events and alcohol drinking. London, England: Longman publishers.

Waltman, C, (2007). The effects of mild ethanol intoxication on the hypothalamic-pituitary-adrenal axis in nonalcoholic men, Michigan, USA: Michigan University press.

Waltman, C, et al (2007). The effects of mild ethanol intoxication on the hypothalamic-pituitary-adrenal axis in nonalcoholic men. Michigan, USA: Michigan University press.

Wand, G.S, et al (2001); Alterations in the hypothalamic-pituitary-adrenal axis in actively drinking alcoholics. Glascow, Scotland: Journal of Clinical Endocrinology and Metabolism, Scotland.

William J. D, (1991); "Psychological Adjustment and Substance Use Among Adolescents Before and After a Parental Divorce," *Child Development*, Vol. 62 pp. 328–337.